Illustrated

Navigation

Ivar Dedekam

2. Edition

Reprinted 2011

fernhurst
BOOKS

Introduction

This book will teach you how to navigate in the traditional way using compass, log and plotter and also how to navigate by means of electronic aids like GPS, radar and chartplotter. In addition you will also learn some basic celestial navigation using the sun and stars to obtain your position using sextant, almanacs, tables and a watch.

Knowlegde of traditional navigation is very important, not only when you have a breakdown of the electronic equipment but also as a means to reveal wrong setups and malfunctioning of this equipment.

What distinguishes this book from the majority is the short, concentrated text backed up by over 120 computer-generated graphics. My aim has been to make it easy to find, understand and remember the information you are seeking. I must also express my thanks to Harald Erik Bjerke for his translation of the original norwegian text.

To the reader and navigator, I wish you Good Sailing and Good Luck!

Ivar Dedekam

Contents

TRADITIONAL COASTAL NAVIGATION

Traditional coastal navigation entails navigation using paper charts, compass, dividers, plotter, log, echosounder and more. **It is important to have a basic understanding of this type of navigation so you can spot malfunctioning or incorrect use of any electronic equipment installed.**

In the next chapter **electronic navigation** *incorporating radar, GPS and electronic charts will be covered. In the last chapter we will show how you can determine your position with the help of sextant, tables and the correct time, using* **celestial navigation**.

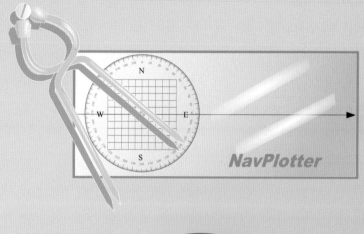

Because the earth is not a perfect sphere, but slightly compressed at the poles, there are problems in creating accurate charts. Many **chart datums** *or* **references** *have been created along the way to describe the not quite spherical earth.*

1

How charts are created

Through the years different **projections** have been used to transfer the contours of the planet earth onto paper. **Mercator** unfolded the sphere like a cylinder and stretched the curved sections so the **meridians** became parallel lines.

This caused the land-masses to be squashed the further they were from the equator. The charts were stretched north south until the land regained the correct proportions.

This is the reason the distance between the parallels of latitude increases the further north or south you go on a Mercator chart. This in turn gives the wrong relationship, size-wise, between the land-masses. Areas far from the equator will seem relatively larger than they actually are.

*Gerardus Mercator (1512-94), Flemish mathematician who projected the earth on to a cylinder, tangent to the earth at the equator.

The curved portions are smoothed and stretched . . . . and the sphere becomes a flat surface.

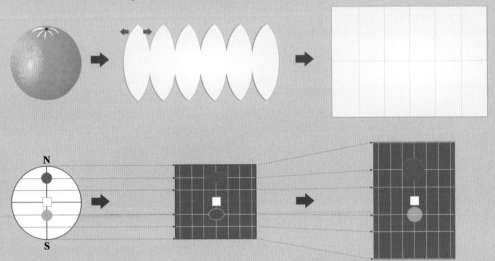

Areas far from the equator appear stretched wider so the chart is stretched higher to compensate . . .

Different types of projections

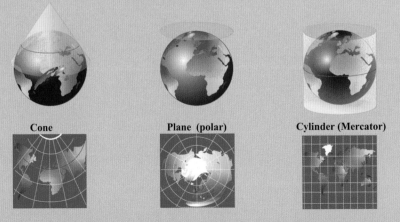

Cone   Plane (polar)   Cylinder (Mercator)

Latitude and longitude

Today's charts use an international reference system consisting of a grid made up of *great circles* and *parallel circles* or just *parallels*.

Parallels

A plane through the centre of the earth will always define a *great circle* on the earth's surface. An example of such a great circle is the *equator* which divides the earth into a northern and southern *hemisphere*. If we slice the earth with planes parallel to the equator we get lesser parallel circles usually called *little circles*.

The equator is a great circle with equal distance to both poles defined as *0° latitude*. The other parallels have increasing latitude reaching 90° at the poles. Latitude is defined as a number of degrees north or south of the equator. N 45° is the parallel halfway between the equator and the north pole.

Meridians

Great circles created by planes at right angles to the equatorial plane which intersect both the north and south poles (and thereby the centre of the earth) make up what we call *circles of longitude*. These circles are divided at the poles and the semicircles are called *meridians*.

For practical purposes the meridians start with the *0-meridian* which goes through the observatory in *Greenwich* near London, = 0° longitude.

The meridians are designated 10°, 20°, 30° etc. *east* and *west* of Greenwich. At 180° the east and west meridians meet at a common meridian. The socalled *date line* runs mostly along the 180° meridian, although in some places it deviates from it due to practical reasons. *When passing the date line, the date must be adjusted.*

This is due to the fact that the earth rotates towards the right (east). A total revolution takes 24 hrs which means 15° an hour. Even though the sun is stationary, it seems to be moving 15° from east to west every hour. The further east you travel the "later in the day" it gets. If you travel far enough to the east you will sooner or later cross the date line and enter "yesterday". If you cross the line from east to west, you have to skip a day.

All this is of little importance in coastal navigation, but very important in celestiall navigation and when using tide tables and nautical tables.

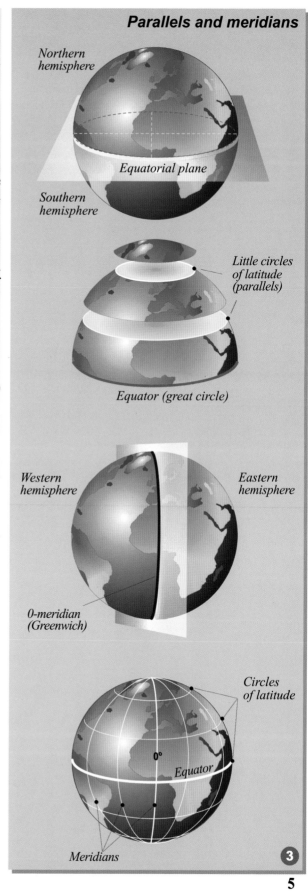

Parallels and meridians

Northern hemisphere

Equatorial plane

Southern hemisphere

Little circles of latitude (parallels)

Equator (great circle)

Western hemisphere

Eastern hemisphere

0-meridian (Greenwich)

Circles of latitude

0°

Equator

Meridians

Position

Any point on the surface of the earth can be defined by its latitude and longitude. The latitude is defined by the parallel that intersects the position and the longitude by the meridian that intersects the position. All places on a parallel circle have the same latitude just as all places on a meridian have the same longitude. But there is only *one unique place* which is defined by the intersection of the two!

The place where you are is called *your position* or the *vessel's position*. When giving our position we always start with latitude and then longitude.

Boat A in the illustration is found to be at latitude 33°N (latitude 33 degrees north) and longitude 45° W (longitude 45 degrees west). The vessel's position would be given thus: 33°N 045°W.

The sailboat B is in the southern hemisphere. Its latitude is 37°S and longitude 18°E. Its position would be referred to as 37°S 018°E.

Here the position is given in whole degrees. This is too generalized for navigation. As shown on page 7 these positions would at least be given in degrees and minutes.
Boat A's position would then be 33°23'N 045°11'W or as it also can be presented, N33°23' W045°11', but either way the latitude comes first.

Latitude is indicated with 2 digits (0-90° N or S) and longitude with 3 digits (0-180° W or E).

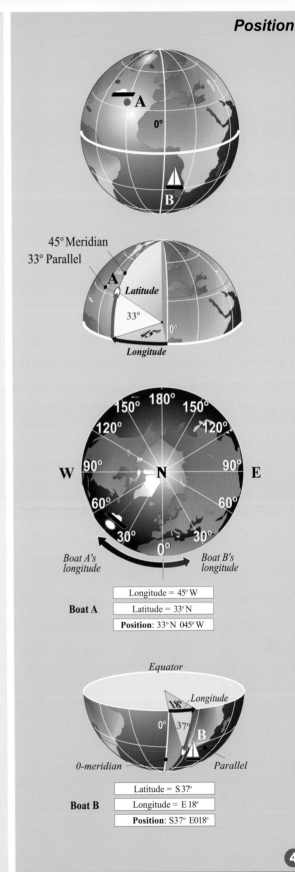

45° Meridian
33° Parallel
A
Latitude
33°
45°
0°
Longitude

Boat A's longitude

Boat B's longitude

	Longitude = 45° W
Boat A	Latitude = 33° N
	Position: 33° N 045° W

Equator
Longitude
18°
0°
37°
B
0-meridian
Parallel

	Latitude = S 37°
Boat B	Longitude = E 18°
	Position: S37° E018°

4

All *circles* may be divided into **360 degrees**. Each degree is divided into 60 **minutes** which in turn can be divided into 60 **seconds**. It is now common to use decimals (tenth of a minute) rather than seconds.

> 1 deg. = 1° = 60 min. (60')
> 1 min. = 1' = 60 sec (60")

Thus:

> 1' 30" = 1 min 30 sec = 1.5 min = 1.5'

You have to keep your wits about you when working with minutes, decimals and seconds.

Nautical mile (M)

One **nautical mile** is defined as 1 **minute of arc** (or 1/60 of a degree of latitude) **measured along a meridian.**

From the equator to the north or south pole there are:
90° = 90x60 = 5400 minutes of arc = 5400'

The great circle is four times that distance:
5400' x 4 = 21600'

As the earth's circumference has been determined to be about 40 000 km = 40 000 000 m:

1 nautical mile = 40 000 000 : 21600 = 1851.85m

This is rounded off:

> 1 nautical mile = 1M = 1852 m

(*A cable* = 1/10 M = 185 m is less frequently used.)

In the example on page 6 the position of a vessel was found to be N33° W45°. A little more accurately it could be defined as N033°23' W045°11' which is read north 33 degrees 23 minutes - west 45 degrees 11 minutes. This is how a position is designated. You could also include decimals of minutes, for example N33°23.7' W045°11.3', if a more accurate position is required.

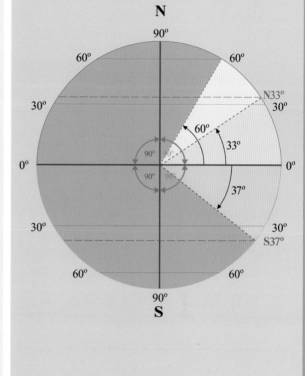

> 1 degree = 1° = 60 minutes = 60'

> Great circle: 4 x 90 x 60' = 360 x 60' = 21600' (minutes)

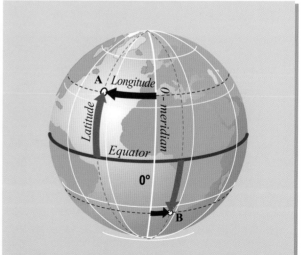

Latitude is the distance in deg. and min. *from the equator.*
Longitude is the distance in deg. and min. *from the 0-meridian.*

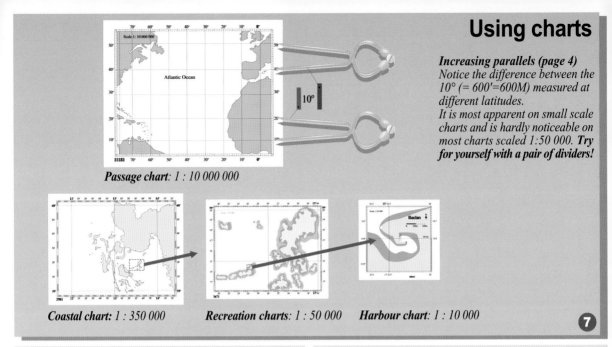

Using charts

Passage chart: 1 : 10 000 000

Increasing parallels (page 4)
Notice the difference between the 10° (= 600'=600M) measured at different latitudes.
It is most apparent on small scale charts and is hardly noticeable on most charts scaled 1:50 000. ***Try for yourself with a pair of dividers!***

Coastal chart: 1 : 350 000   *Recreation charts: 1 : 50 000*   *Harbour chart: 1 : 10 000*

7

When navigating you will be using charts with varying *scales*. The scale defines how much a distance is reduced on the chart. 1:50 000 is a scale found on many charts. 1mm on this chart equals 50 m (50 000 mm) in the terrain. Other charts like *harbour charts* and *special charts* might have a scale of 1:10 000 or 1:25 000. *Coastal charts* with a scale less than 1:200 000 and *passage charts* with a very small scale are often used. N.B. 1:10 000 is a larger scale than 1:350 000.

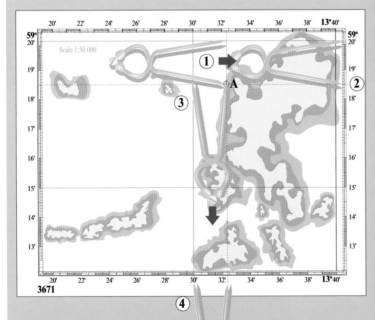

3671

4

Defining a position on the chart

1. Place the dividers on the closest line of latitude or another horizontal line. Open until the other leg is on your position.
2. Move the divider out to the scale on the fringe of the chart with the point on the horizontal line and note the latitude.

Latitude: **59° 18.5' N**

3. Place the dividers on the closest meridian or another vertical line. Once again open until the other leg is on your position.
4. Move the dividers up or down to the longitude scale with the point on the line and note the longitude.

Longitude: **013°32.4'E**

A's position: 59° 18.5'N, 013°32.4'E

*NB! The longitude increases to the right because the area on the chart is **east** of Greenwich.*

8

You can determine a position on the chart by drawing a horizontal line from the position to the edge of the chart and reading off the latitude. Draw a vertical line from the position (up or down) and read off the longitude on the scale. However, most people choose to use dividers to measure the distance from the closest horizontal or vertical line and then move the dividers along these lines out to the fringes in order to read off latitude and longitude.

There are several ways to define your position, just make sure you read off where lines through your position, parallel with the edges of the chart, intersect the latitude and longitude scales.

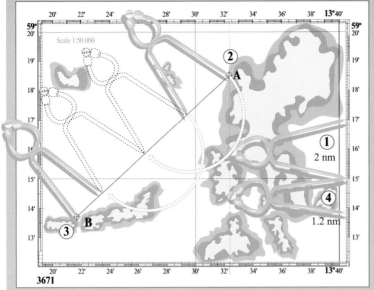

Measuring the distance from A to B

1. You could measure the distance in one go if the dividers are big enough. The most common method is to measure a whole number of nautical miles on the latitude scales on the right or left side of the chart.

2. Place one leg of the dividers on A and "walk" the dividers as close to B as you can.

3. Measure whatever is left with the dividers.

4. Move the dividers to the scale and find the distance and then work out the total distance.

$$\text{Distance} = 3 \times 2M + 1.2M = \underline{7.2M}$$

Try working out this distance in other ways.

9

You can measure the distance with whatever you please but dividers are most commonly used. *Always* use the *latitude scale* on the left or right side level with the area between A and B. This is because the minutes of latitude increase with increased latitude, even if it is hardly noticeable on a 1 : 50 000 scale chart. Try this on different charts until you are sure you understand the problem.

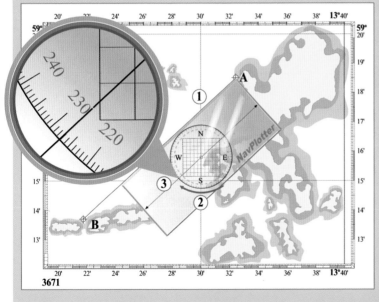

Take the bearing from A to B

1. Lay the plotter along the line from A to B trying to get a meridian, or a line parallel to it, visible in the adjustable compass rose (preferably in the centre).
2. Turn the rose until it lines up with the meridian or any parallel line, making sure **N** is up.
3. Note the course **227°** on the rose.

10

You will now have found the course from A to B which you can steer the boat by. There are many types of navigational plotter which can be used (explained later). This is the main principle in traditional navigation - how to sail from one point (A) to another (B). When the course is set, is it just a matter of steering according to the compass and keeping track of your progress on the log? *No!*

In the real world you have to make corrections for many inaccuracies and discrepancies like compass variation and deviation, current, wind and tide amongst others. This we will deal with further along in the book!

Variation and deviation

The ***magnetic north pole*** is situated in northern Canada as this is written, but it is continuously and slowly moving around in these northerly areas. ***Variation*** is the difference in degrees the compass is showing in reference to ***true north***. If the magnetic north pole had coincided with the geographical, the compass needle would always point towards the north pole along the meridian through your position. The variation may be really high sometimes in some places! ***Always check the chart and calculate the current variation in the area*** (fig.18).

Deviation

The compass is also affected by local disturbances from the boat where it is mounted. Iron and steel on board create ***magnetic fields***. Electrical circuits and loudspeakers create ***electromagnetic fields*** which also cause the compass needle to deviate from the magnetic north pole. This is what we call ***deviation***. Deviation alters with ***course*** (and heeling), but also over time. Far too many recreational skippers fail to take deviation into account. This is a practice which could have serious consequences in situations where one is totally reliant on the compass, like in thick fog.

NB! Some of the deviation can be eliminated by adjusting the compass with the built in correction magnets, something which should be done by experts.

Take every opportunity to check deviation! Write down a deviation table!

Even if you are not able to set up a complete table, it is necessary to note down the deviation for the main directions so as to give an indication of the inaccuracy of the compass. A quick and easy way to set up a table is given below.

Handbearing compass method

Go out on a day with calm water and position yourself on board in a place with little or no deviation. This will differ from vessel to vessel, but on a boat with stainless stays (non-magnetic), all the way aft could be a good place. Get the crew to steer the main headings on the main compass while you note the course on the handbearing compass. You could get a table as shown in the figure. You can also draw up a deviation graph as shown.

Note how the deviation changes in relation to changes in course. The engine often has a large effect. On the figure at the bottom you see how it attracts the compass needle in the simplified situations shown.

In principle, every time you are sure of your true course (when on a leading line, for example) figure out your deviation just to verify.

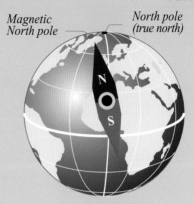

Magnetic North pole

North pole (true north)

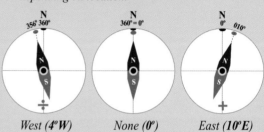

Variation is ever changing and differs depending on location.

West (4°W) None (0°) East (10°E)

Deviation *is how much the boat's own magnetic field pulls the compass needle away from* ***magnetic north***.

West (8°W)

Compass course	Deviation
000° (N) =360°	8° W
023° (NNE)	7° W
045° (NE)	6° W
068° (ENE)	4° W
090° (E)	2° W
113° (ESE)	0° W
135° (SE)	4° E

Course: 270° Dev.: 3°E

Course: 90° Dev.: 2°W

Correction for variation and deviation

Due to the fact that the **magnetic** north pole and the **geographical** (true) north pole do not coincide, you need to know different ways to define a heading:

TH - True heading *(no variation or deviation)*

MH - Magnetic heading *(variation)*

CH - Compass heading *(both variation and deviation)*

Westerly variation and deviation is defined as **minus**.

Easterly variation and deviation is defined as **plus**.

---

*When converting **towards true heading**, in other words from **CH** to **MH** or **MH** to **TH**, you **subtract** **westerly** and **add easterly** variation and deviation. Therefore **keep the sign**.*

---

*When converting **away from true heading**, in other words from **TH** to **MH** or **MH** to **CH**, you **add westerly** and **subtract easterly** variation and deviation. **Change sign:** + to - and - to +.*

If you are going from one place to another, e.g. from A to B as on p.9, you first determine the **true heading** from the chart = 227°T. Then you have to correct for variation which in this example is 2°W or -2°. If the deviation for this course is 6°E, we end up with the following calculation:

TH =		227° T
var =	+	2°
MH =		229° M
dev =	-	6°
CH =		223° C

This means that if you want to go from A to B you have to steer 223° on your steering compass. In addition you have to compensate for wind and current as shown later in this book.

The examples below are a little exaggerated in order to make it easier to understand. Many prefer to memorize the three rules on the left rather than to rely on reason when going from TH to CH or opposite.

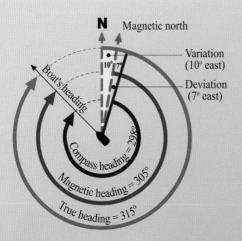

Example 1:

CH =	298° C
dev =	+ 7°
MH =	305° M
var =	+ 10°
TH =	315° T

Keep sign — *Change sign*

Variation =10° E, Deviation=7° E

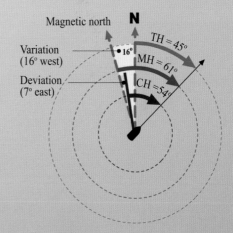

Example 2:

CH =	54° C
dev =	+ 7°
MH =	61° M
var =	- 16°
TH =	45° T

Keep sign — *Change sign*

Variation =16° W, Deviation=7° E

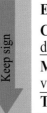

12

Steering compass

The three classic instruments available to the navigator are the *log* (speed/distance), *echosounder* (depth) and *compass* (heading). The compass is the most important because without visible references, you are lost if you don't have this instrument.

The *magnetic compass* has functioned in the same way for hundreds of years. A magnetic needle is suspended in a housing filled with alcohol or oil. The needle will always attempt to point towards the *magnetic north pole*. The earth can be viewed as a large magnet where the magnetic poles vary from the geographical poles as described on p. 10.

Originally the *compass rose* was not divided into numbers. The seamen of old had to remember 32 headings, half of which you can see on the illustration. Each *quarter* was divided into 8 sectors - 32 sectors all together (1 sector = 11¼°).

Other compass types

There are other types of compass besides the magnetic. The *flux-gate compass* uses the *electromagnetic field* surrounding the earth. Instead of permanent magnets it makes use of coils and require electrical supply to operate.

The earth's magnetism induces a weak current in the coils which can be electronically measured and *displayed*. *Autopilots* often use this type of compass. You can pre-adjust the compass for variation and most compasses will compensate for deviation after turning the vessel 360°.

The *gyrocompass* is found on all larger vessels but is not so well suited for leisure craft due to high cost and size. In addition it needs electricity to work. The gyrocompass makes use of the inertia of a spinning wheel ring and orients itself to true north. It works independently of magnetic forces so it has no variation or deviation due to iron or steel.

The magnetic compass is the most reliable as it is not reliant on electricity. All certified vessels are required to have at least one magnetic compass on board.

Handbearing compass

A handbearing compass can be either magnetic or flux-gate. The latter has the ability to *store* several bearings which can be retrieved on demand.

The deviation of the handbearing compass is not known. For this reason you place yourself where the deviation is minimal, usually in the bows or in the stern on boats with stainless stays (non-magnetic).

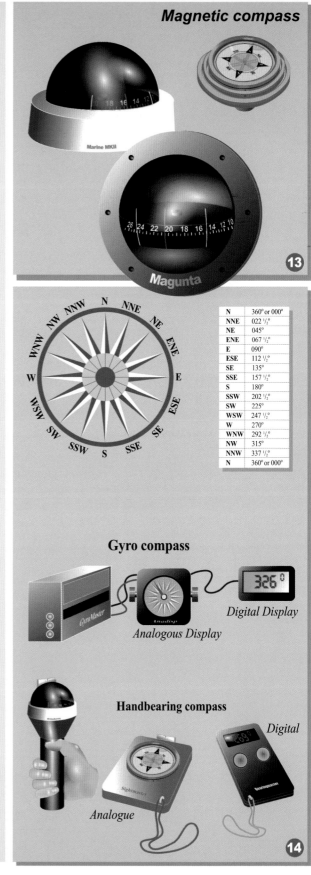

Magnetic compass

N	360° or 000°
NNE	022 ½°
NE	045°
ENE	067 ½°
E	090°
ESE	112 ½°
SE	135°
SSE	157 ½°
S	180°
SSW	202 ½°
SW	225°
WSW	247 ½°
W	270°
WNW	292 ½°
NW	315°
NNW	337 ½°
N	360° or 000°

Gyro compass

Digital Display

Analogous Display

Handbearing compass

Digital

Analogue

The log

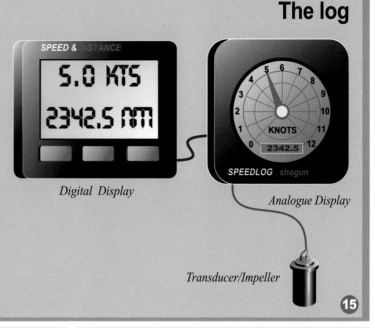

N.B. The majority of logs indicate the speed of the water over the hull, or as we say, the boat's *speed through the water*.

If the boat is heading *into* a 5 kn current and not making headway, the log will still show a boat speed of 5 kn. The opposite is the case if heading *with* a current. The log would maybe show 2 kn while the boat would be doing 7 kn *over ground* with a following current of 5 kn.

There are logs where the transponder is placed inside the hull without moving parts. They make use of the *Doppler effect* and measure true speed over the ground.

All logs have to be thoroughly calibrated in order to give accurate readings.

Digital Display

Analogue Display

Transducer/Impeller

15

Log as in a piece of wood. A piece of wood attached to a line with knots at given intervals was thrown over the side. The navigator counted how many knots ran out over time, measured by an hourglass. Thus the term *knot* indicating 1 nautical mile an hour. Modern logs measure the speed of the water using an *impeller* mounted in a *'through hull'* fitting. The electronics figure out distance and speed.

The echo-sounder

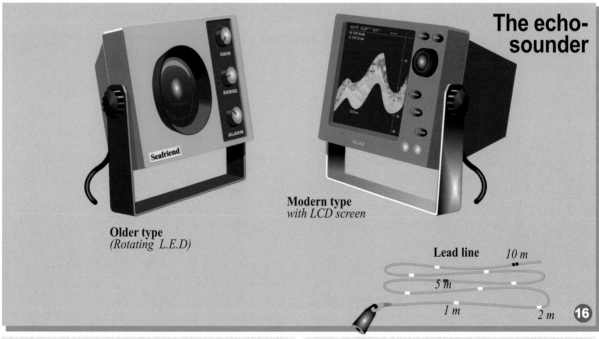

Older type
(Rotating L.E.D)

Modern type
with LCD screen

Lead line   10 m

5 m

1 m

2 m   **16**

The *echo-sounder* can be of great use when navigating, especially in fog and reduced visibility. Along with chart and compass you can use the soundings to determine your position. At slow speeds you could use a *lead line* made with a line and weight. For practical reasons measurable depth is limited. The echosounder sends sound waves down towards the bottom and measures the time it takes for the sound to return. The instrument works out the depth based on this. The part sending out the pulse is called the *transducer* and is usually placed in the bilges. Echo-sounders can show the *water depth* or the *depth below the keel*. There are echo-sounders which can see forward and to the sides, but these are not covered here.

Plotting implements

There are many types of plotting implement. The most well known is the *parallel ruler*, but it is best suited for use on larger vessels with a large stable chart table. On board a recreational vessel a *plotter* with a compass rose might be a better choice.

You place the north-south line of the rose parallel with a meridian (vertical line on the chart) and the ruler along your course line. Your heading is indicated by the intersection of the ruler and the compass rose.

The parallel ruler must be moved from your course line to the centre of the closest rose on the chart as shown in the figure. The heading is indicated where the ruler cuts through the rose. ***The problem with the parallel ruler, besides needing a rose on the chart, is that it has a tendency to skid and twist when walking it in a small boat in rough seas.***

The final choice is yours. Some navigators just use a couple of 45° angles which they slide along each other. Electronic plotters of various kinds are also available.

Sharpened *pencils* (no harder than HB), *pencil sharpener*, *eraser* and *magnifying glass* are included in the tools needed for chartwork. A magnifying glass is often needed to pick out details in a small scale chart. Keep in mind that on a 1:50000 chart, 1mm signifies 50m! A small island shows up as a dot which is easily confused with a pencil mark.

Compass roses

Many charts are embossed with a *compass rose* to aid in setting a course. The rose is usually double with a rose showing *true heading* (TH) and one rotated with the variation showing *magnetic heading* (MH). The variation is indicated on the rose, in this figure: 6°W 2001 (8'E).

This means that the variation changes 8 minutes (8') eastward every year. The variation would be about 5°W in 2008 (decreases: 8'x7=56' which is about 1°).

When setting a course on the chart, always use the outer rose.

When you wish to derive true course from magnetic course, use the inner rose and read the result on the outer rose. The opposite when you wish to find magnetic course from true course.

Examples: 0° magnetic corresponds to 354° true (1).
240° magnetic corresponds to 234° true (2).
136° true corresponds to 142° magnetic (3).

NB! This is only correct in the year indicated on the rose.

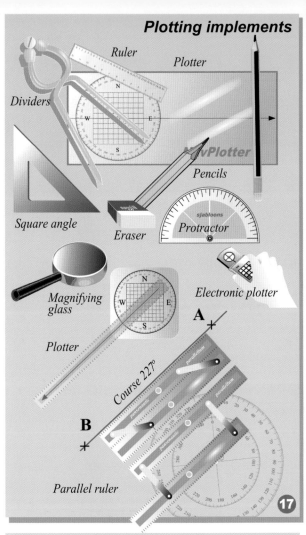

Plotting implements

Ruler
Plotter
Dividers
NvPlotter
Pencils
Square angle
Eraser
Protractor
sjabloons
Magnifying glass
Electronic plotter
A
Plotter
Course 227°
B
Parallel ruler

17

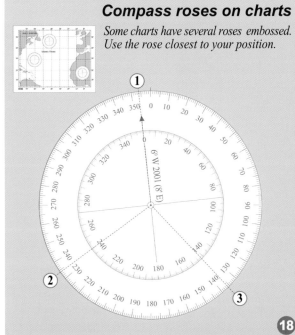

Compass roses on charts

Some charts have several roses embossed. Use the rose closest to your position.

① 6° W 2001 (8' E)
②
③

18

Leeway and current

You have to correct your course for *leeway* (drift) and *offset* due to wind and current. The leeway is due to wind and must be corrected towards the wind. When we talk about wind direction we mean where the wind is coming from. Westerly and southerly winds come *from* the west and south, respectively. *When referring to currents it is the opposite! A northerly current moves to the north and a westerly current moves to the west.*

The leeway due to wind is a matter of strength and direction. Rule of thumb has it that you correct 1° for every 2 knots (= 1 m/s) of wind when beating in a sailboat. This is a very general indication and you should get to know your own vessel as each boat has a different leeway in the same conditions.

In our example the true course from A to B was 227°. If the wind was from NW blowing 20 kts, we would deduce from experience that the drift would be 10°. We would have to sail 10° *closer* to the wind in order to sail our course.

	Course from chart	= 227° T
+	**drift**	= 10°
	= **Course to steer**	= 237° T

If the wind had been from the south you would have subtracted 10° from both true heading and compass heading.

Current

There are several different kinds of currents. Large *ocean currents* like the Gulf Stream, *wind generated currents*, *currents from rivers* and *tidal currents* which we will deal with later. Currents can be complicated but on most occasions you have to make corrections for current.

If you know the speed and direction of the current you can calculate your *course over the ground* as shown in the figures (more on this in fig. 52 and 53).

In our example there is a easterly current of 2 kts and you are steering 227°T doing 5 kts, your course over ground will be 208°T. *The course over the ground will be your track along the seabed.*

Very often, when the direction and strength of the current is known, you want to know what course to steer in order to achieve a *certain course over the ground* as shown in fig. 53.

The easiest scenario is if the current is directly **with** or **against** you. This will not affect the boat's course. The speed over the ground will be speed on the log **minus** the speed of the opposing current.

With a *following current* the speed over the ground will be speed on the log *plus* the speed of the current.

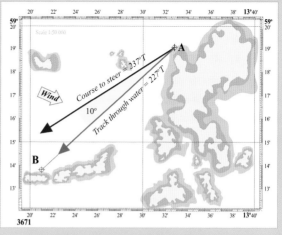

Course to steer = 227° + 10° = 237°T

(CH must be adjusted as well.)

When drawing vector diagrams:
Course through water is marked with 1 arrow
Course over ground is marked with 2 arrows
Tide or current is marked with 3 arrows

Draw your course steered as a line in the right direction using 1 cm or nm for every knot of speed (1-2).
Draw the current from the end of course steered in the same way (2-3). Speed and course over ground appears as a line from 1-3. You notice that the boat will move off the course line due to the current.

Current

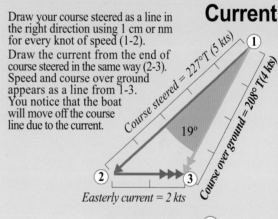

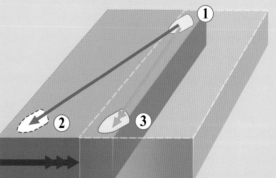

*The boat sails through the water from 1 to 2. At the same time the block of water the boat is sailing in has moved from 2 to 3, **with the current**. Thus the course over the ground is 1-3.*

19

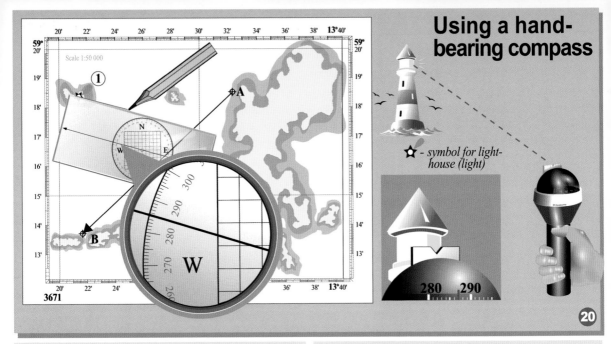

☆ - *symbol for light-house (light)*

En route from A to B you want to make sure you are *on your intended track*. You could take a cross bearing with a *handbearing compass*. Pick out a fixed object like the light (1) and take its bearing by aiming at it with the bearing compass. Read off the bearing from the compass card. In this example: **287°C**. N.B. Getting an accurate fix can be difficult in a sea. You should take several bearings and work out the average. Modern electronic compasses have this function built in.

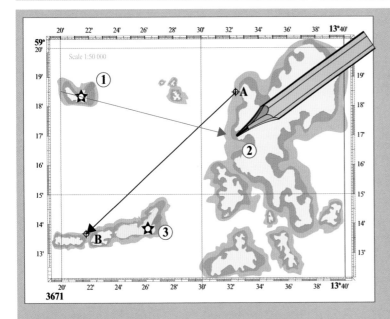

N.B. You have to make adjustments for variation. Deviation is considered nil as the bearing compass is kept away from the engine and anything else made of iron and steel.
Let's assume variation 2°W:

Compass bearing	CB:	287°C
Deviation	Dev:	0°
Magnetic bearing	MB:	287°M
Variation	Var:	- 2°W
True bearing	**TB:**	285°T

When converting from **CB** to **TB** we use *minus* for **W** and *plus* for **E** variation and deviation.

Place the plotter through the *observed object* (light) setting the angle to 285°T while keeping its vertical lines parallel with a meridian. Draw a line through the light to a point (2) on the other side of the course line. We call this line a *position line*. You are somewhere on this line because your bearing to the light is 285°T. You do not, however, know where on this line you are. You can take another bearing, for example to the **light** (3). *N.B. It's important that the two bearings are as close to right angles to each other as possible.*

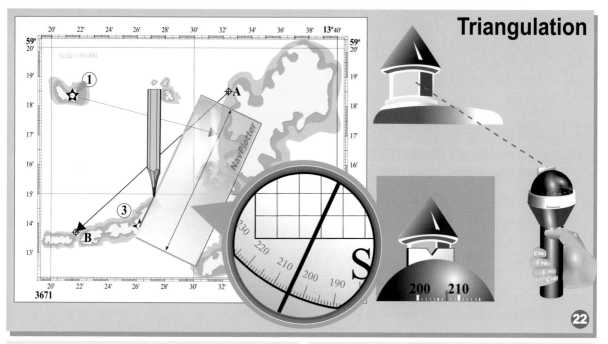

The bearing to the next light is **205°T**. Place the plotter through this light (3) setting the angle to 205°T while keeping its vertical lines parallel with a meridian and north up. Draw a line *through* the light, along the ruler until it intersects the first position line. You now have a *new position line*. You have to be somewhere along this line as well. *Your position will be where the two position lines intersect (4)! You should always use three position lines 60° apart, if possible, as shown on the next figure.*

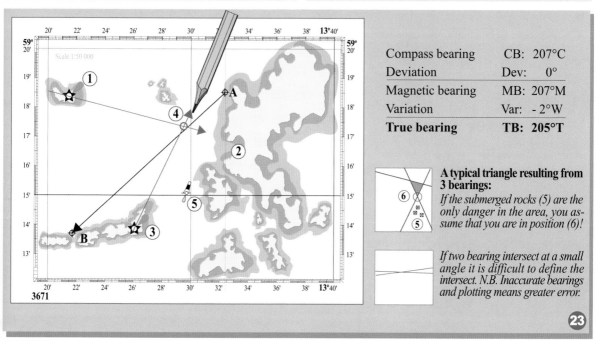

Compass bearing	CB: 207°C
Deviation	Dev: 0°
Magnetic bearing	MB: 207°M
Variation	Var: - 2°W
True bearing	**TB: 205°T**

A typical triangle resulting from 3 bearings:

If the submerged rocks (5) are the only danger in the area, you assume that you are in position (6)!

If two bearing intersect at a small angle it is difficult to define the intersect. N.B. Inaccurate bearings and plotting means greater error.

To be on the safe side you should take a third bearing to the *West marker* (5). N.B. Avoid using floating markers when taking a bearing as they may have drifted off their charted position (but use them with caution if there is nothing else to take a bearing on). *You will always end up with a triangle* when taking three bearings (the bearings will never be accurate enough). To be on the safe side, always assume you are in the *worst corner* of the triangle in respect to possible danger (rocks, shallows, reefs, ...) nearby. *N.B! It's possible, though more difficult, to take bearings with the steering compass. You must then make corrections for the deviation for the boat's course at every bearing made.*

Determining position from one point (the running fix)

Often you only have one point to take a bearing to along a coast. You assume you are at position 1 and take a bearing to the light at 330°T and draw it on the chart. You know you are somewhere on this *position line*. You read off the log 255 M and sail along your course line until you reach position 2 where you note the bearing to the light as 50°T and read off the log 261 M. The bearing is drawn on the chart and you have a new position line which you are on. *N.B. Ideally the two bearings should be at 90° to each other.*

Distance travelled, 261-255 = 6 M, is marked off along the course line from point 1. This distance is moved parallel to your course line until it fits between the bearing lines.

Pos. 3 is your new *observed position. This method is not very accurate, especially if tspeed and direction of an eventual current is unknown!*

45° bearing

First take a bearing to the light (3) when it is 45° *on the bow* (1) and read off the log. Note the log when the bearing is 90° on the bow and find logged distance. The triangle 1-2-3 is a **90°-45°-45° triangle** which means that the distance to the light (3) from your position (2) is the same as logged distance 1-2.

The distance to the light when abeam is equal to distance logged between bearings.

NB! This method is inaccurate if there is significant current or leeway. (You can also take the bearings in opposite order, first 90° abeam, then 45° off the stern.)

One bearing and distance

When closing on a shore *at night* you may *spot the light* from one of the large coastal lighthouses on the horizon. If you take a bearing on it *just as it appears* you can find the distance from a table and obtain a relatively good observed position.

In this example the bearing to the light is 75°T. You draw your position line 1-2 through the lighthouse as shown in the fig. *The height of the light* is 18m (59') and your height of eye is around 4m (13').

From the tables in the fig. you find the distance to be 13M. Draw the segment of a circle with radius 13M from the light. Observed position is where the circle intersects position line 1.

General rule of thumb for distance in miles (M):

$$\text{Distance} = 2 \times (\sqrt{h_1} + \sqrt{h_2})$$

h_1=height of eye, h_2=height of object

(heights in meters)

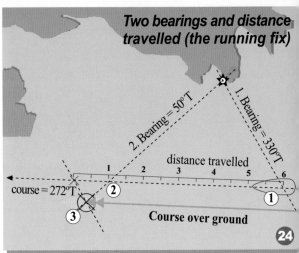

Two bearings and distance travelled (the running fix)

2. Bearing = 50°T

1. Bearing = 330°T

distance travelled

course = 272°T

Course over ground

24

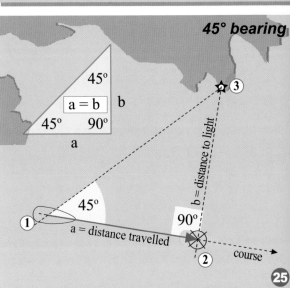

45° bearing

$a = b$

a = distance travelled

b = distance to light

course

25

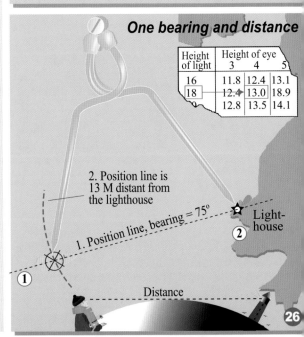

One bearing and distance

Height of light	Height of eye 3	4	5
16	11.8	12.4	13.1
18	12.4	13.0	18.9
	12.8	13.5	14.1

2. Position line is 13 M distant from the lighthouse

1. Position line, bearing = 75°

Light-house

Distance

26

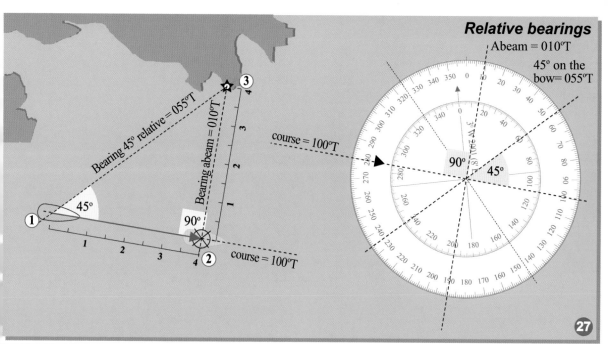

Abeam = 010°T

45° on the bow= 055°T

Bearing 45° relative = 055°T

Bearing abeam = 010°T

course = 100°T

course = 100°T

90°

45°

In the example in figure 25 you were to take a 45° bearing on the light and then 90° on your centre line, so called *relative bearings*. You can create fixed marks on board for this purpose, or you can figure out the appropriate *true bearings* using the chart rose.

Your true heading (TH) = 100°T. Your bearing 45° on the bow would be TB = 100 - 45= 55°T and abeam TB = 100 - 90= 10°T. (If you had been going in the opposite direction heading 280°T you would have got TB = 280 + 45= 325°T and TB = 280 + 90=370=10°T.)

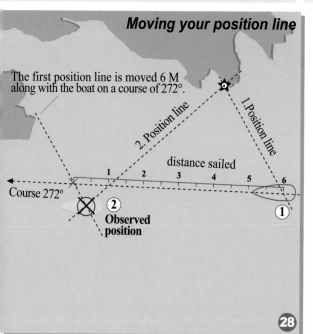

Moving your position line

The first position line is moved 6 M along with the boat on a course of 272°.

2. Position line

1.Position line

distance sailed

Course 272°

Observed position

In the example in fig. 24 you can arrive at your position by *moving* the first position line along *with the boat*. You know that you are somewhere on the first position line, but not exactly where, as you take your bearing. When you take your next bearing, the boat has sailed a certain distance on a certain course. If you move the first position line the same distance

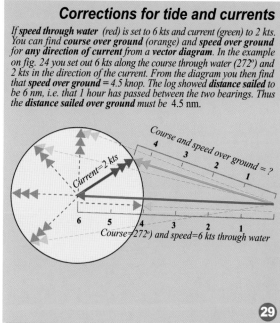

Corrections for tide and currents

*If **speed through water** (red) is set to 6 kts and current (green) to 2 kts. You can find **course over ground** (orange) and **speed over ground** for **any direction of current** from a **vector diagram**. In the example on fig. 24 you set out 6 kts along the course through water (272°) and 2 kts in the direction of the current. From the diagram you then find that **speed over ground** = 4.5 knop. The log showed **distance sailed** to be 6 nm, i.e. that 1 hour has passed between the two bearings. Thus the **distance sailed over ground** must be 4.5 nm.*

Course and speed over ground = ?

Current=2 kts

Course=272°) and speed=6 kts through water

and course you must still be somewhere on this line! At the same time you must be somewhere on the *new* position line. *Observed position is therefore at the intersection of the two lines.* This is a technique much used in navigation. *NB! You always have to make necessary corrections when speed and direction of the current are known.*

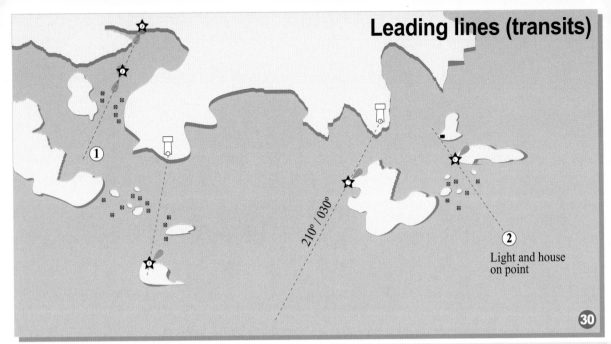

Leading lines (transits)

210° / 030°

② Light and house on point

Leading lines (transits) of all kinds are useful aids in navigation, both for determining your position as well as guiding you clear of dangers such as shoals and other obstacles (1 and 2). Along with lights, buoys and day-marks you can use towers, churches, buildings and other conspicuous objects. Just make sure the mark you see is the mark on the chart. You can also use islands and other natural formations, once again making sure they correspond to what you see on the chart.

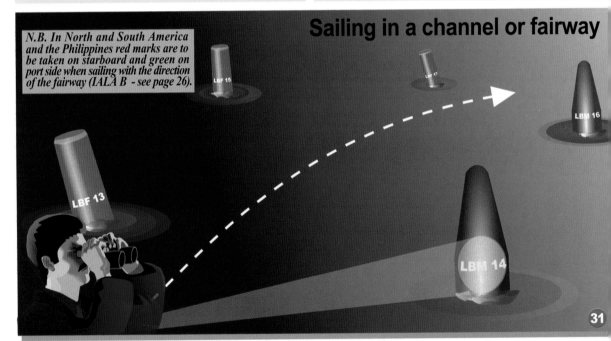

Sailing in a channel or fairway

N.B. In North and South America and the Philippines red marks are to be taken on starboard and green on port side when sailing with the direction of the fairway (IALA B - see page 26).

LBF 15 LBF 17 LBM 16 LBF 13 LBM 14

It is very important, especially at night, to verify that the marks you observe are the ones you think they are. When following a winding channel, verify the numbers and markings on the red and green buoys as you pass them. Use a torch and binoculars if necessary. Beware of a current which could put you on one of them. A fairway is often marked with red and green markers, lateral marks. When sailing with the direction of the channel or fairway, red marks should be taken on port and green on starboard (they should coincide with the colour of the navigation lights). Opposite when sailing against the direction of the channel or fairway. Always refer to the chart where traffic direction of the fairway is usually indicated (fig. 44).

Some chart symbols

In addition to the symbols in the IALA-system, shown on page 26-27, there are several chart symbols you should be familiar with. ***These symbols vary from country to country***. Here are shown some of the most important ones. Complete descriptions can be found as supplement listings to charts. ***Examples:***

In UK: CHART 5011: Symbols and abbreviations used on Admiralty charts.
In the US: Chart No. 1: Nautical Chart Symbols Abbreviations and Terms

Depth indication: Older charts use fathoms, but all references will ultimately be given in meters in UK. ***In the US and the waters around, fathoms and feet are still used. Always check the chart!***
Blue tint in one or more shades is used to show depth limits according to scale and use of the chart. On older charts various dotted lines are used.
Drying areas, exposed at low tide, are usually shown as a green area.
Isolated shallows are marked with a cross at its highest point. The depth is noted next to it, usually in cursive.
Depths of less than 5m with little detail were often bordered by a dotted line on older charts.
Depth contours enable a visual indication of the bottom.
Overhead cables are normally noted with minimum clearance at ***high tide***.
Bridges are also indicated with vertical clearance normally above high water (alway check the chart!).

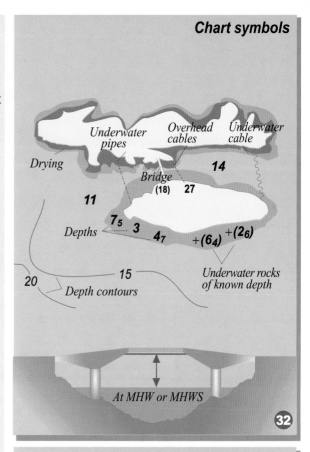

Coversion table Fathoms to Meters (on nearest whole foot)

Meter	0.0	1.0	2.0	3.0	4.0	5.0	6.0	7.0	8.0	9.0	10.0
0.0	0_0	0_3	1_1	1_4	2_1	2_4	3_2	3_5	4_2	5_0	5_3
0.1	0_0	0_4	1_1	1_4	2_1	2_5	3_2	3_5	4_3	5_0	5_3
0.2	0_1	0_4	1_1	1_5	2_2	2_5	3_2	4_0	4_3	5_0	5_3
0.3	0_1	0_4	1_2	1_5	2_2	2_5	3_3	4_0	4_3	5_1	5_4
0.4	0_1	0_5	1_2	1_5	2_2	3_0	3_3	4_0	4_4	5_1	5_4
0.5	0_2	0_5	1_2	1_5	2_3	3_0	3_3	4_1	4_4	5_1	5_4
0.6	0_2	0_5	1_3	2_0	2_3	3_0	3_4	4_1	4_4	5_2	5_5
0.7	0_2	1_0	1_3	2_0	2_3	3_1	3_4	4_1	4_5	5_2	5_5
0.8	0_3	1_0	1_3	2_0	2_4	3_1	3_4	4_2	4_5	5_2	5_5
0.9	0_3	1_0	1_4	2_1	2_4	3_1	3_5	4_2	4_5	5_2	6_0

Example from table: 6.6 m = 3_4 = 3 fathoms 4 feet

More accurate: 1 fathom = 6 feet = 1.83 m
 1 foot =12 inches = 0.305m 1"= 0.0254 m

This gives more accurately:
6.6 m : 6.6/1.83 = **3 fathoms** + rest: 6.6 -(3x1.83) = 1.11 m
1.11m :1.11 / 0.305 = **3 feet** + rest :1,11m-(0.305x3)=0.20 m
0,20 m :0.20 /0.0254 = **7.68" Total: 3 fathoms 3 feet 7.68"**

N.B! *Always check the charts thoroughly before use. They contain lots of information! The colours/shades may vary depending on the make of cartography. Generally heights are shown above MHWS in the UK. In the US they are shown above mean high water, MHW, which may make a significant different when tidal ranges are large!*

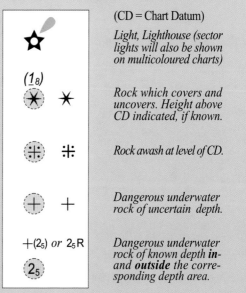

(CD = Chart Datum)

Light, Lighthouse (sector lights will also be shown on multicoloured charts)

Rock which covers and uncovers. Height above CD indicated, if known.

Rock awash at level of CD.

Dangerous underwater rock of uncertain depth.

Dangerous underwater rock of known depth ***in-*** *and* ***outside*** *the corresponding depth area.*

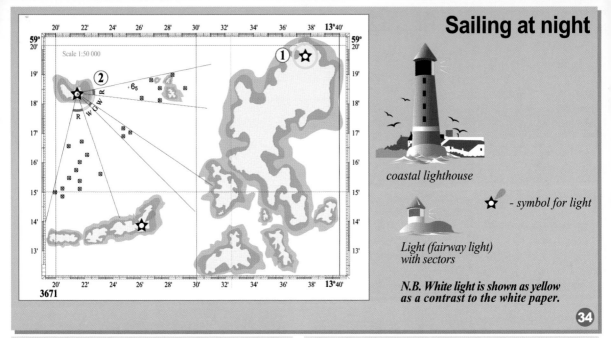

Sailing at night

coastal lighthouse

☆ - *symbol for light*

Light (fairway light)
with sectors

N.B. White light is shown as yellow
as a contrast to the white paper.

34

When closing on a shore in the dark, you usually first see one of the *big lighthouses* (1) with 360° sweep and unique characteristic. Further along these will be substituted by *smaller lighthouses* with *sector lights*. Inshore you will encounter many lights on shore along with *fixed* and *floating marks* with a light mounted on top. Lights in the same area usually have *different characteristics* in order to distinguish them. Further on the characteristics can be repeated.

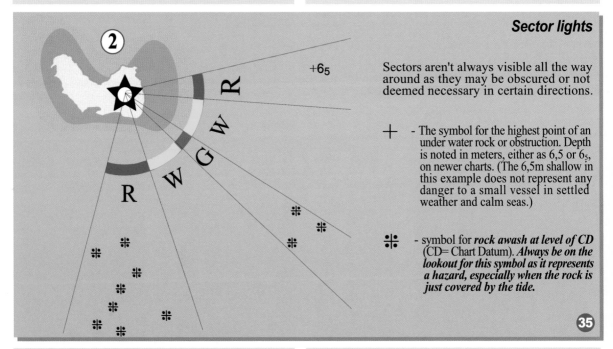

Sector lights

Sectors aren't always visible all the way around as they may be obscured or not deemed necessary in certain directions.

$+$ - The symbol for the highest point of an under water rock or obstruction. Depth is noted in meters, either as 6,5 or 6_5, on newer charts. (The 6,5m shallow in this example does not represent any danger to a small vessel in settled weather and calm seas.)

- symbol for *rock awash at level of CD* (CD= Chart Datum). *Always be on the lookout for this symbol as it represents a hazard, especially when the rock is just covered by the tide.*

35

Sector lights show white (W), red (R) and green (G) light in precisely defined sectors. *White* is the *only secure sector*. If you find yourself in red or green sector indicating foul water, the chart will tell you which way to alter course in order to get back into the white sector. Recreational vessels and small craft can often sail in red and green sectors. You must find out from the chart where the dangers are located. Red and green sectors often mark areas deep enough for smaller vessels in calm weather. *Crossing shallow areas in rough seas is always a risk in rough weather. N.B. Hazards can occur in white sector!*

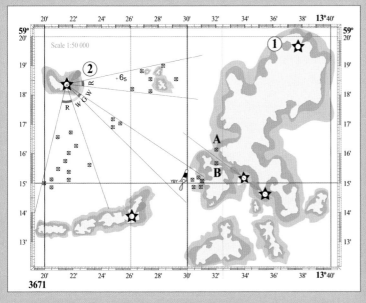

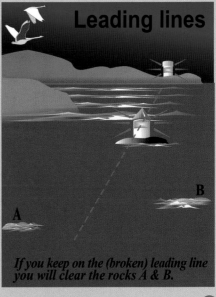

Leading lines

If you keep on the (broken) leading line you will clear the rocks A & B.

Leading lines are often used instead of sectors in narrow channels when precision is required. **Leading marks** are shown in the chart along with a line showing where it is safe to sail. **Leading lights** are used in the dark, showing fixed or flashing white, red or green light. Standard lights can be used as well as long as they have different characteristics and the one furthest away is higher.

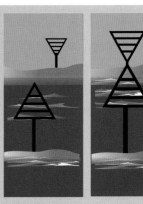

Alter course to starboard!

Here the light furthest away appears to port. Therefore change course to starboard.

Alter course to port!

Here the light furthest away appears to starboard. Therefore change course to port.

Perfect! Steady as she goes!

Turn to port! Steady as she goes!

Here the mark furthest away appears to starboard. Therefore change course to port.

Leading lines are always given as a true heading which makes it possible to check the *deviation* of the compass as mentioned earlier. Steer the leading line and read off the compass course. Figure out the deviation after having adjusted for the variation which you find on the chart, and compensating for any cross-tide. Which way should you turn if the two lights or marks are not aligned? *Steer to the opposite side of where the furthest mark or light appears to be.*

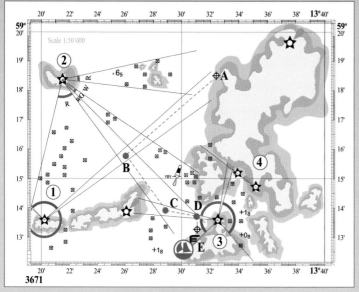

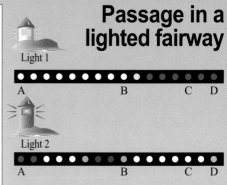

Light 1

A ● ● ● ● ● ● ● ● ● ● ● ● ● ● ● ● ● ● B ● ● ● ● C ● D

Light 2

A ● ● ● ● ● ● ● ● ● ● ● ● ● ● ● ● ● ● B ● ● ● ● C ● D

N.B. You can tell when you are in the fringes of a white sector. The light will turn slightly red or green depending on which fringe you are on. Check the chart! You will be on the separation between sectors and you have a position line! But keep in mind that if it's misty this line can be inaccurate.

38

You're on passage from A to the **marina** E in total darkness. First you sail in the white sector from light (1) after making sure, (double check) that you are looking at the right light with the **correct characteristics**. **Beforehand** you have also identified light (2) by its characteristics. You sail in **white sector** from light 1 while you observe the sectors from light 2 change from red to white to green. When you enter light 2's **next white sector**, you turn about 90° to port and sail SE in this sector. At this point you should have

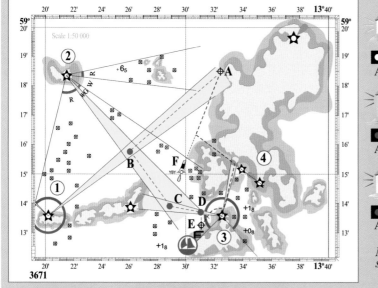

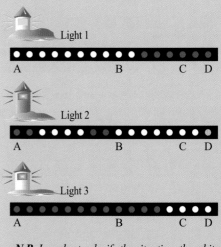

Light 1

A ● ● ● ● ● ● ● ● ● ● ● ● ● ● ● ● ● ● B ● ● ● ● C ● D

Light 2

A ● ● ● ● ● ● ● ● ● ● ● ● ● ● ● ● ● ● B ● ● ● ● C ● D

Light 3

A ● ● ● ● ● ● ● ● ● ● ● ● ● ● ● ● ● ● B ● ● ● ● C ● D

N.B. In order to clarify the situation, the white sectors are coloured yellow in this picture!

39

identified light 3's special characteristics! You continue in the white sector from light 2 until you see light 3 change from red to white (C). You then sail towards light 3 until you see the entrance lights to the south of your position (D). Go south to E and enter the marina. **This is the safe way to sail from A to E but there are other alternatives!** If you go from A towards the west marker (F) until you can identify the leading lights (4), you can steer through the narrow sound on the leading lights until you reach the white sector from light 3. Approach the light cautiously in white sector eventually keeping it to port until you see the entrance lights to the marina.

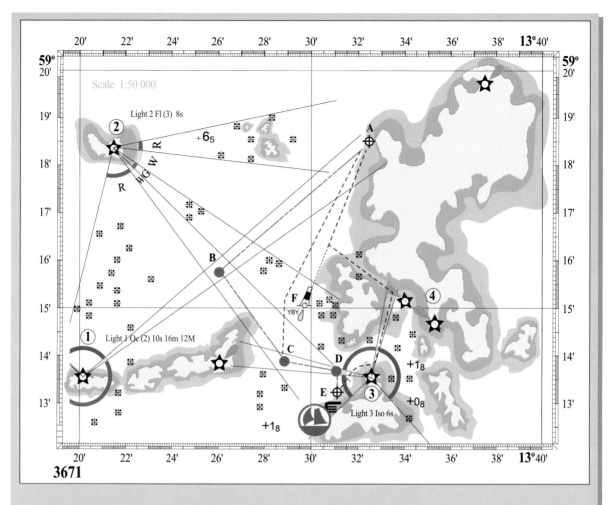

Characteristics

Group-Occulting: A fixed light is turned off the number of times indicated in parenthesis (otherwise 1). In this example we have two dark periods every 10 seconds. Use a stop watch or count 1001, 1002, 1003... Count from one incident until the same incident reoccurs.

Group-Flashing: Darkness is interrupted by number of flashes indicated in parenthesis (otherwise 1). In this example we have a group of three flashes repeated every 8 seconds.

Isophase: Iso means equal in greek. Light and dark periods are equal and are repeated every 6 seconds in this example.

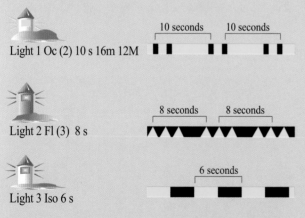

Light 1 Oc (2) 10 s 16m 12M — 10 seconds | 10 seconds

Light 2 Fl (3) 8 s — 8 seconds | 8 seconds

Light 3 Iso 6 s — 6 seconds

An easier route (green) is to approach the *west marker* (F), *pass to the west* of the mark continuing south to (C) and follow the directions given earlier. There are usually several options but the safest is to navigate using the sectors. Floating markers might have drifted or been hit by other vessels.

A light's *characteristics* are noted on the chart following the name of the light. *Light 1*, for example, is followed by Oc (2) 10s 16m 12M, where Oc (2) is the characteristic and 16m is the hight of the light source in meters above sea level. 12M is the maximum distance in nautical miles the light is visible in optimum conditions.

IALA buoyage system

IALA (**A**) system for buoys is common for most countries. However in **South** and **North America** and the **Philippines** they use the IALA (**B**) system where the red and green **lateral buoys** have they **colours** reversed, not their shapes.

The cardinal buoys in the two systems do not differ and indicate **safe passage** in the direction of the buoys name. In other words **it is safe to pass to the west of a west buoy or marker**!

Lateral buoys are used to **mark a fairway** in and out of harbour. In European waters you keep red to port and green to starboard when sailing in the direction of the fairway. Opposite of course, when sailing **against** the direction of buoyage (noted on your chart) or sailing in South and North America or the Philippines.

Both lateral and cardinal buoys can vary in shape as shown in the next picture. The colour coding, however, is always the same. The chart symbols may vary from country to country. Buoys may have **lights** for identification at night. **Keep in mind that buoys may drift. N.B. Topmarks are often omitted!**

A: NORTH MARKER (cardinal buoy)
Greatest depth **to the north** of the mark. Hint: Topmark points up/north. Black on top = north.
When lit (white): continuous quick/very quick
Reflecting tape: 1 blue + 1 yellow below

B: SOUTH MARKER (cardinal buoy)
Greatest depth to **the south** of the mark. Hint: Topmark points down/south. Black down=south.
When lit (white): 6 quick + 1 long every 15 sec. or 6 very quick + 1 long every 10 sec.
Hint: 6 flash = 6 o'clock = south
Reflecting tape: 1 yellow + 1 blue below

C: EAST MARKER (cardinal buoy)
Greatest depth to **the east** of the mark.
Hint: Yellow in middle = sunrise = east.
When lit (white): 3 quick every 10 sec. or 3 very quick every 5 sec.
Hint: 3 flash = 3 o'clock = east
Reflecting tape: 2 blue

D: WEST MARKER (cardinal buoy)
Greatest depth to **the west** of the mark.
Hint: Black in middle = sunset = west
When lit (white): 9 quick every 15 sec. or 9 very quick every 10 sec.
Hint: 9 flash = 9 o'clock = west
Reflecting tape: 2 yellow

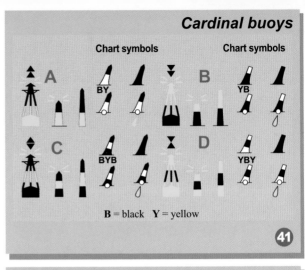

Cardinal buoys

Chart symbols   Chart symbols

B = black   **Y** = yellow

41

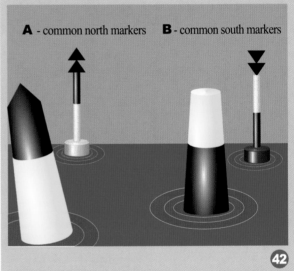

A - common north markers   **B** - common south markers

42

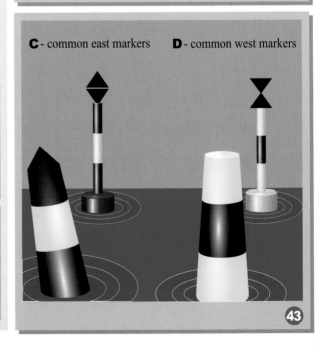

C - common east markers   **D** - common west markers

43

Lateral buoys are used to *mark fairways* and entrances to harbours. In European waters you keep *red to port* and *green to starboard* when sailing in the direction of the fairway. (Colours coincide with your navigation lights).

F: PORT MARKER (lateral buoy)
The red port markers are *left to port* when sailing in the direction of the fairway.
When lit: red with any characteristic
Reflecting tape: red

G: STARBOARD MARKER (lateral buoy)
The green starboard markers are *left to starboard* when sailing in the direction of the fairway.
When lit: green with any characteristic
Reflecting tape: green

I: ISOLATED DANGER
Clear on all sides. Used for isolated rock or danger.
Buoys with lights: 2 white group flash
Reflecting tape: 1 blue + 1 red below

H: CENTER FAIRWAY
Clear on all sides. Used for marking middle of channel or as general nav aid.
When lit: 2 white oc or long flash every 10 sec.
Reflecting tape: 1 red + 1 white below

J: SPECIAL
Marks special places like beaches and recreational areas.
When lit: yellow with any characteristic
Reflecting tape: yellow

Buoys are anchored to the bottom. Small craft can on occasion pass on the "wrong" side of a buoy. In restricted areas or areas with a lot of traffic it could be wise to go on the "inside" of some marks.
Always check the depth on the chart!

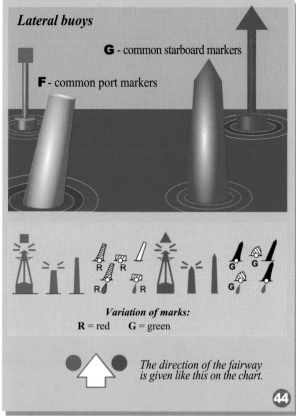

Lateral buoys

G - common starboard markers
F - common port markers

Variation of marks:
R = red   G = green

The direction of the fairway is given like this on the chart.

44

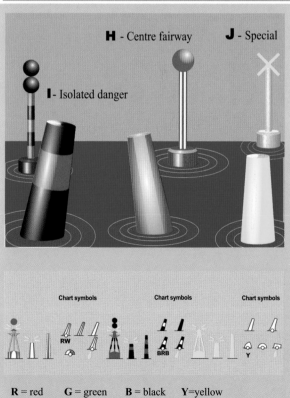

H - Centre fairway   **J** - Special
I - Isolated danger

Chart symbols   Chart symbols   Chart symbols

RW   BRB   Y

R = red   G = green   B = black   Y=yellow

45

Tides

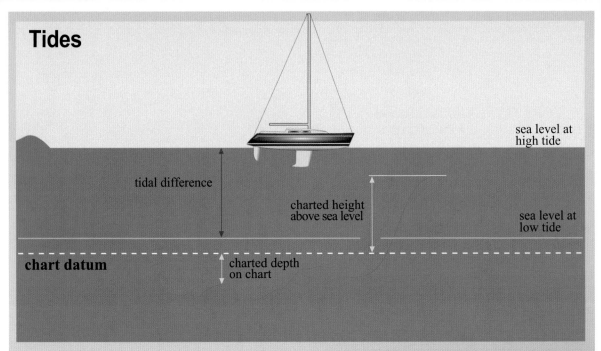

sea level at
high tide

tidal difference

charted height
above sea level

sea level at
low tide

chart datum

charted depth
on chart

Tide is caused by the moon's and sun's motion *in reference to* the earth. Other heavenly bodies affect the tide as well but it is primarily the moon circling the earth which "pulls" the water due to its gravitational force. The sun, which is much larger but further away, acts as an amplifier when the sun and moon are lined up.

The level of tide is noted in tables as height above *chart datum*. Chart datum varies in different countries but is often lowest possible tide. This means that you most often have a little extra under your keel. The times for high and low tide change approx. 50 min. each day as the daily moon phase is 50 min. longer than the sun phase. You can calculate about 12 hrs. and 25 min. between each high water. *This is handy to know if you are without a tide table.*

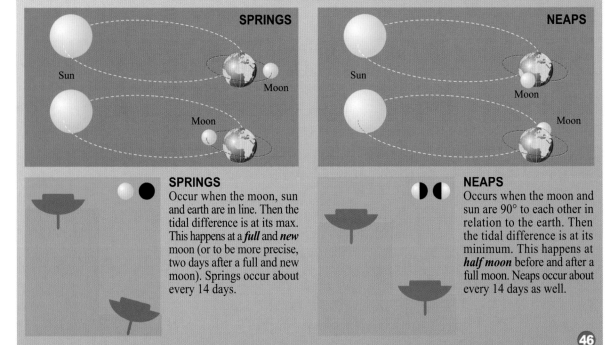

SPRINGS

NEAPS

Sun

Moon

Moon

Sun

Moon

Moon

SPRINGS
Occur when the moon, sun and earth are in line. Then the tidal difference is at its max. This happens at a *full* and *new* moon (or to be more precise, two days after a full and new moon). Springs occur about every 14 days.

NEAPS
Occurs when the moon and sun are 90° to each other in relation to the earth. Then the tidal difference is at its minimum. This happens at *half moon* before and after a full moon. Neaps occur about every 14 days as well.

46

Tide tables

Tide tables give you times for high and low water every day of the *designated year*. In addition they contain the height of the tide. The tables contain data for important harbours called *standard ports*. Examples are Dover, Brest and Cuxhaven.

What is the level of tide at Dover when the time is 11:30 in a time zone 2 hours ahead of UTC on May 17, the year designated in the table shown?

Times in the table are UTC (= GMT). *Always check what time reference is being used! It can be a good idea to have a watch on board set to UTC!*

Converted to UTC the time is: 11:30-2 = 09:30 UTC

The table shows the closest high water is 12:31 UTC and the height is 6.9 m. 09:30 is about 3 hrs before high water. In the tidal curve below right you will find a *factor* of about *0.55*.
Multiply the *range*, difference between high and low water, by this factor and add it to the low water figure.

High water	12:31 UTC	= 6.9 m
- Low water	07:50 UTC	= 0.6 m
= Range		= 6.3 m
Low water	07:50 UTC	= 0.6 m
+ 6.3 m x 0.55		= 3.5 m *(rounded up)*
= Height	09:30 UTC	= 4.1 m

Rule of thumb says that the water level changes by 1/12 the first hour, 2/12 the second, 3/12 the third, 3/12 the fourth, 2/12 the fifth and 1/12 the sixth hour (total 12/12) from high water to low water and low water to high water.

3 hours before high water would be:

$$3/12 + 2/12 + 1/12 = 6/12 = 0.5$$

Using 0.5 as our factor:

Low water	07:50 UTC	= 0.6 m
+ 6.3m x 0.5		= 3.2 m *(rounded up)*
Height	09:30 UTC	= 3.8 m

Which doesn't deviate much from what you got when using the tidal curve!
There are other applications which give more accurate results but often it is good enough to use the rule of thumb while giving yourself a little to go on. It should be used very carefully in areas with islands or shallow water.

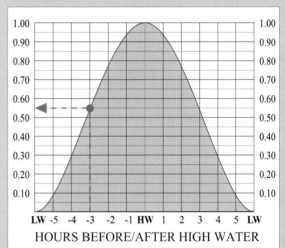

TIME ZONE UT (GMT)   **DOVER**
LAT 51°07'N LONG 1°19'E

MAY

	Time	m		Time	m	
1 M	0712	1.0	**16** TU	0704	0.5	Low water
	1208	6.5		1143	6.9	High water
	1921	1.1		1924	0.6	
2 TU	0023	6.5	**(17)** W	0005	7.0	Date
	0735	1.1		0750	0.6	Height in meters
	1240	6.5		1231	6.9	Time
	1944	1.1		2010	0.6	
3 W	0051	6.4	**18** TH	0055	6.8	
	0759	1.2		0836	0.7	
	1309	6.4		1321	6.8	
	2011	1.2		2058	0.7	
4	0114	6.2	**19**	0147	6.6	
	0826	1.3		0923	0.9	

Tidal curve

HOURS BEFORE/AFTER HIGH WATER

The tidal ranges differ a lot depending on where you are. Some places it is negligible while in the English Channel and Brittany it can be up to 12 m! In these areas it is important to know at least when high and low water occur.

N.B. *The level of tide derived from tables is not the actual depth but has to be **added to the depth** given on the chart.*
Note that: HW = high water and LW = low water
See p.36 for the use of graphs for Standard Ports included in many Tide Tables.

47

Standard Port DOVER <---

RAMSGATE
LAT 51°19.5'N LONG 01°25.6'E

1. Because high water in Dover is 12:31 we use the correction which is the closest (makes no difference in this case).

2. Because high water in Dover is 6.9 m we must choose this correction.

MHWS = Mean High Water Spring

Times				Height (metres)			
High water		Low water		MHWS	MHWN	MLWN	MLWS
0000	0600	0100	0700	6.7	5.3	2.0	0.8
1200	1800	1300	1900				
① **Difference RAMSGATE** ③				②			④
+0020	+0020	-0007	-0007	-1.8	-1.5	-0.8	-0.4

3. Because LW Dover is 07:50, we use the closest correction (makes no difference in this case).

4. LW Dover is 0.6 m and this correction is used.
MLWS= Mean Low Water Spring

For May 17 we have:

High water Dover:	1231 UTC	6.9 m		Low water Dover:	0750 UTC	0.6 m
Correction Ramsgate:	+ 0020	-1.8 m		Correction Ramsgate:	- 0007	- 0.4 m
High water Ramsgate :	1251 UTC	5.1 m		Low water Ramsgate:	0743 UTC	0.2 m

48

What is the tide in Ramsgate on May 17?
The time of high and low water can vary substantially within a 5 M area. The tables would be impractical if they were set up for every harbour and anchorage. For this reason standard ports are used as reference for a long list of *secondary ports* indicating time and height *corrections*. **N.B.** These correction tables may vary in appearance depending on which almanac you use.

Enter a harbour with a charted depth of 0.8 m:
The boat draws 2.0 m. You want a *margin of 1 m* under your keel (minimum depth = 3m). Can you enter the harbour 3 hrs after HW (HW + 3) at 11:00?
From a table you get: HW 07:50 - 4.2 m/LW 13:18 - 0.6 m
-Tidal range = 4.2 m-0.6 m=3.6 m
-3 hrs after HW gives factor: 1/12+2/12+3/12=6/12=0.5
-Tide will have fallen 3.6 x 0.5 = 1.8 m
Minimum depth (HW+3) = 0.8+ (4.2-1.8) = 3.2 m

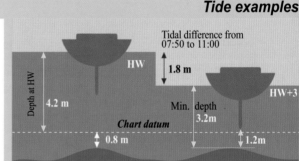

Anchoring example: At 08:00 you have anchored in 5.5 m and the boat draws 2.0 m. Will you have enough water under the keel at low water?
From a table you get: HW 06:11 - 5.1 m/LW 12:38 - 1.1 m
-Tidal range = 5.1 m - 1.1 m = 4 m
-2 hrs after HW gives factor: 1/12+2/12=3/12=1/4
-Tide will have fallen 1/4 x 4=1 m and will fall another 3 m.
Depth under the keel at LW = 5.5 - 3.0-2.0 = 0.5 m

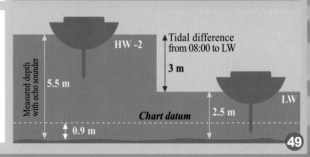

49

Figuring out the correct level of tide can seem daunting. The effect of *barometric pressure* and *wind* may add a *big factor of inaccuracy* (tidal heights are only *predictions*). *You should at least be able to determine the state of tide at any given time for any given place.* If you follow the examples on this page, you should be able to keep it simple as long as you *give yourself* *a good margin of safety!* Remember, charted depths are noted in the chart. Height of tide must be *added* to the charted depth! Even at low tide you will have a little extra water in your favour. Charted depths are LAT (Lowest Astronomical Tide) which is the lowest possible level. *Refer to the tables and give yourself a good margin!*

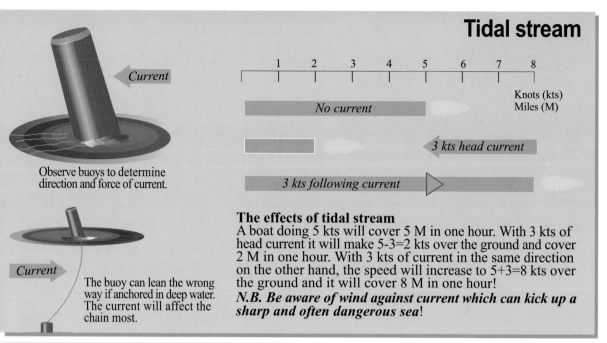

Tidal stream

Observe buoys to determine direction and force of current.

The buoy can lean the wrong way if anchored in deep water. The current will affect the chain most.

No current

3 kts head current

3 kts following current

Knots (kts)
Miles (M)

The effects of tidal stream
A boat doing 5 kts will cover 5 M in one hour. With 3 kts of head current it will make 5-3=2 kts over the ground and cover 2 M in one hour. With 3 kts of current in the same direction on the other hand, the speed will increase to 5+3=8 kts over the ground and it will cover 8 M in one hour!
N.B. Be aware of wind against current which can kick up a sharp and often dangerous sea!

Areas with large tidal range and channels can experience strong tidal streams. In the English Channel one can experience tidal streams in excess of 7 kts. It is therefore important to know the direction and strength of the current in order to avoid problems.

There are special *tidal stream charts* and you can often find information about the current on the chart. It's important to check buoys constantly to determine direction and force of the current because charts and tables aren't always correct.

Tidal stream charts & tables

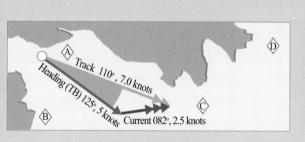

Track 110°, 7.0 knots

Heading (TB) 125°, 5 knots

Current 082°, 2.5 knots

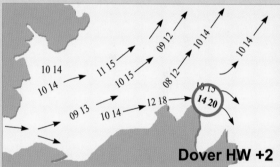

Dover HW +2

Tidal Streams referred to HW at Dover

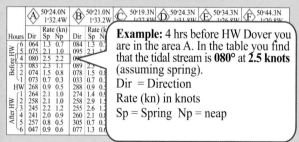

	(A) 50°24.0N 1°32.4W		(B) 50°21.0N 1°33.2W		(C) 50°19.3N 1°27.8W		(D) 50°24.3N 1°31.8W		(E) 50°34.3N 1°26.8W		(F) 50°44.3N 1°29.8W	
		Rate (kn)		Rate (k								
Hours	Dir	Sp	Np	Dir	Sp	N	Dir					
Before HW 6	064	1.3	0.7	084	1.3	0.						
5	075	2.1	1.0	095	2.1							
4	080	2.5	2.2	09								
3	083	2.3	1.1	089	2.3							
2	074	1.5	0.8	078	1.5	0.						
1	073	0.7	0.3	033	0.7	0.						
HW	268	0.9	0.5	288	0.9	0.						
After HW 1	264	2.1	1.0	274	1.4	0.						
2	258	2.1	1.0	258	2.9	1.						
3	245	2.2	1.2	255	2.6	1.						
4	241	2.0	0.9	260	2.1	0.						
5	257	0.8	0.5	305	0.7	0.						
6	047	0.9	0.6	077	1.3	0.						

Example: 4 hrs before HW Dover you are in the area A. In the table you find that the tidal stream is **080°** at **2.5 knots** (assuming spring).
Dir = Direction
Rate (kn) in knots
Sp = Spring Np = neap

Tidal stream charts give you direction and speed of tidal stream every hour, 6 hours before and after high water at a standard port (here two hours after HW Dover).
Choose a stream chart that is closest to the time in relation to HW Dover. Read off the speed (the arrow shows the direction) as in this example:
Stream: *1.4 knots* at *neap* and *2.0 knots* at spring

(51)

Some charts give tidal stream information. The *Tidal Diamonds* marked A, B, C, and so on are positions where you can find information about the tidal stream. You must know when HW occurs in the standard port designated in the table. Read off the information adjacent to the number of hours before or after under the appropriate "diamond".

Tidal stream charts can be found in dedicated books in addition to *nautical almanacs*. They also refer to HW at a standard port. Tides are complex and information gained from charts and tables aren't always correct. Without a GPS it can often be difficult to determine the effect of the current on your *course over ground* (COG) = *track*.

Tidal stream vectors

Determining course over the ground

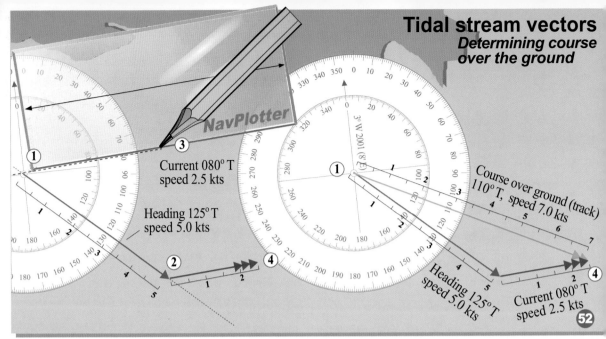

Current 080° T
speed 2.5 kts

Heading 125° T
speed 5.0 kts

Course over ground (track)
110° T, speed 7.0 kts

Heading 125° T
speed 5.0 kts

Current 080° T
speed 2.5 kts

When you know the speed and direction of the current you can calculate your *course over the ground* which is what you need to know. Draw your *true heading* in the rose (1-2) and mark the boatspeed along this line. You can use 1cm =1 knot as a unit. Draw the direction of the current in the rose (1-3) and mark the speed 1cm = 1 knot. Move this line parallely to the end of your bearing line (2). Draw a line from the centre of the rose to the end of the current which will be the *course (track) and speed over the ground* (1-4).

Determining course to steer

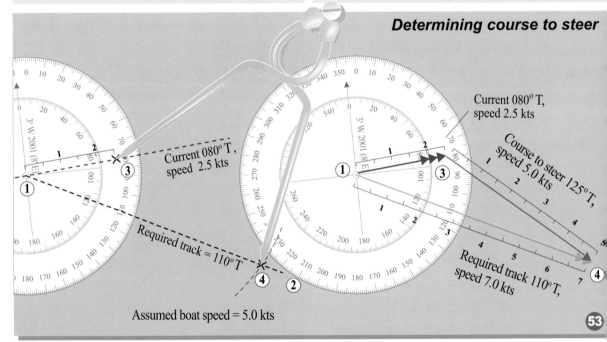

Current 080° T,
speed 2.5 kts

Required track = 110° T

Assumed boat speed = 5.0 kts

Current 080° T,
speed 2.5 kts

Course to steer 125° T,
speed 5.0 kts

Required track 110° T,
speed 7.0 kts

Quite often you wish to know what *course to steer* in order to achieve a certain *track* when you know the direction and speed of the current. Draw the required track (1-2). Draw the direction and speed of the current (1-3). Set the dividers to represent the boat's speed, here 5 kts. Make an arc from 3 to cut the reqired track at 4. The line from 3 to 4 will then be your *course to steer* in order to achieve your *required track*. At the end remember to correct your *heading* for *leeway*. You can use any unit for speed as long as it is used on all lines/vectors. You can use the unit for 1 M on the lat. scale on the edge of the chart as 1 knot if you wish.

Interpreting navigation lights

It's important to know the *different lights* used on vessels and how to define what you see in the dark, as this will influence navigational decisions.

Keep in mind that *nav lights are fixed, not flashing!* (One of the few exceptions is the flashing light on a hovercraft). Thus lighthouses and other lights on stationary objects flash in order to create a *characteristic*.

You will often encounter many confusing lights together. Sort them out. Figure out which ones are boats (the ones moving) and which ones can represent a problem. *Look for the sidelights* which indicate *speed through the water!* Use the following rules:

Boats showing *green sidelight* on your *"green side"* (starboard side) and *red sidelight* on your *"red side"* (port side) will most probably not be on a collision course with you.

Concentrate first on all *red* sidelights on your "green side" and then the *green* sidelights on your "red side".

N.B. If you see a vessel showing red and green sidelights at the same time, it's heading straight for you!

In the illustration at the top, B, C and D are potential dangers as they are showing red on your green and green on your red, while A will go clear (red on red).

Vessel B can only be a sailboat under sail (green sidelight without a steaming light) while the two masthead lights indicate a tug C is crossing your path. Vessel D is the tow. Keep clear!

You also have to familiarize yourself with how a vessel is *turning*, something often encountered with fishing vessels. The two masthead lights will indicate this as shown on the illustration on the right.

All vessels have a white sternlight except for tugs which show an additional *yellow stern light* as shown in fig. 57. So when you *only see* one white fixed light it is usually either a sternlight, a vessel less than 50 m in length at anchor or a boat less than 7 m in length.

N.B. Be aware that it is very difficult to determine distance at night, especially with sailing vessels displaying a tricolour (all three sectors together at the head of the mast).

Motor vessels over 50 m are required to show **two** masthead lights while underway, the forward lower than the aft. N.B. Vessels less than 50 m *may* show two masthead lights but are not required to do so.

Tugs are required to show two masthead lights, one above the other. If the tow is more than 200 m, the tug is required to show three masthead lights above each other.

Sailboats less than 20 m in length may show *"combined"* navigation lights, either red/green on the mast or in the bow or a "tricolour" at the top of the mast.

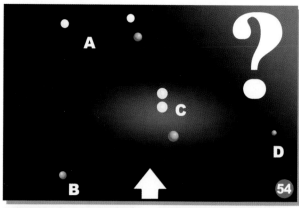

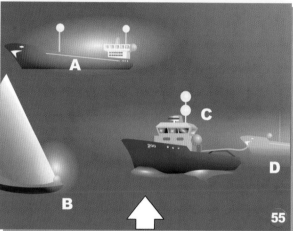

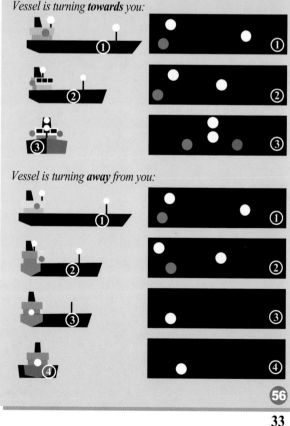

*Vessel is turning **towards** you:*

*Vessel is turning **away** from you:*

Navigation lights for a variety of vessels

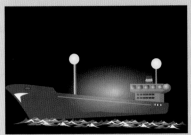

Motor vessel, length greater than 50 m

Vessel under power* (in this case a sailboat)

**Sailboat ** seen from starboard and straight ahead

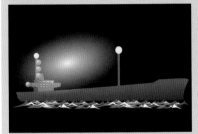

Vessel constrained by its *draught*

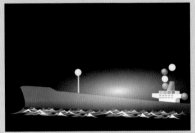

Vessel with *reduced manoeuvrability*

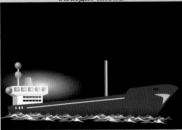

Vessel *not under command*

Fishing vessel *not* trawling

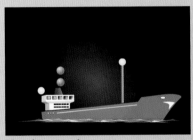

Vessel *aground*

Fishing vessel *trawling*

Pilot vessel * in operation

Tug * with tow less than 200 m

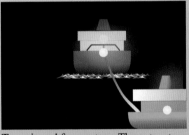

Tow viewed from astern. The extra stern light on the tug is yellow!

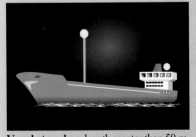

Vessel at anchor, length greater than 50 m

Vessel * *at anchor*

Vessel engaged in *underwater operations*. Vessel should be passed on the "green" side.

57

Review

True heading (TH) = no variation/deviation
Magnetic heading (MH) = TH $\pm$ variation
Compass heading (CH) = MH $\pm$ deviation

***Westerly** variation and deviation is defined as **minus**.*
***Easterly** variation and deviation is defined as **plus**.*

It's easy to make a mistake here. Try ***"chart to compass - add west"***, or even better, visualize/ understand the process.

From chart to compass (TH ➡ MH ➡ CH):
When converting from chart to compass you add westerly and subtract easterly variation and deviation. Change sign: + to - and - to +.

From compass to chart (CH ➡ MH ➡ TH):
When converting from compass to chart you subtract westerly and add easterly variation and deviation. Therefore use the same sign.

You won't always have to go through all these steps. But the setup is there so you can refer to it as a model or reference. Remember to give yourself extra room if you assume no leeway or current.

Examples

var = 5° W, dev = 6°E

TH	120°	▼
± dev	-6° (E)	
MH	114°	
± var	+5° (W)	
= CH	119°	

Visualize it like this:

*5° variation to the west means the compass needle is pulled to the west. It actually points to 355° while it "pretends" to be pointing straight north. If you want to travel **north** you have to steer 000°+5= 005° on the compass. **Add W variation when transferring from TH to CH**.*

CH	116°	▼
± var	-5° (W)	
MH	111°	
± dev	+6° (E)	
= TH	117°	

*When steering north by the compass you are actually tracking 355° on the chart. **Subtract W variation when transferring from CH to TH**.*

CH	116°	▼
± var	-5° (W)	
MK	111°	
± dev	+6° (E)	
= TH	117°	
± leeway	+11°	
= TTW	128° T	

*In this example let's assume it is blowing Force 6 from NNE and you assume the leeway to be 11°. In other words your **track through the water, TTW**, is greater than your heading. If there is no current, **track through the water(TTW)** is equal to **track over ground (TOG)** or **course over ground (COG)** as it is also called. If there is a current use the current vectors to figure out your track.*

TTW	128°	▼
± leeway	-11°	
= TH	117°	
± var	+5° (W)	
= MH	122°	
± dev	-6° (E)	
= CH	116°	

*If you wish to achieve a certain **true track through the water**, lets say 128°, the opposite sign is used as in the bottom box. You figure out the CH needed to achieve a certain track.*

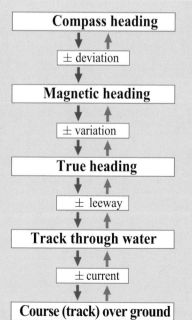

Compass heading
↓ ↑
± deviation
↓ ↑
Magnetic heading
↓ ↑
± variation
↓ ↑
True heading
↓ ↑
± leeway
↓ ↑
Track through water
↓ ↑
± current
↓ ↑
Course (track) over ground

↓ Minus for West and plus for East
Use signs!

↑ Plus for West and minus for East
Use opposite signs!

The easiest calculation is defining

Compass heading = Track

Thus ignoring deviation, variation, leeway and current. You should be able to this if there is no noticeable variation in the area, deviation is unknown and there is no wind or current to speak of.

Minimum correction should be for variation which can be substantial in some areas.

Far too many sailors are not aware of the deviation on their steering compass! This could be of great importance if you do not have other aids such as GPS, radar or other electronic nav aids when the fog closes in!

Using graphs included in Tide tables for Standard Ports

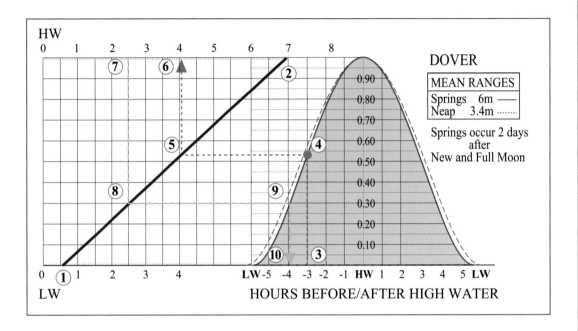

FIND TIDAL HEIGHTS

(see example on page 29)

1. Mark the height of LW on the LW-scale.
2. Mark the height of HW on the HW scale, and draw a line (blue) from point 1 to 2.
3. Enter the Time scale at -3 hours and draw a vertical line up from it.
4. Where this line meets the curve for spring tide, draw a horizontal line.
5. Where this line meets the blue line, draw a vertical line up (or down) to the height scale.
6. Find the height at 3 hours before HW = **4.1 m**.

- *Correct for local time zone/summer time.*

- *If it is spring tide use solid line graph.*

- *If it is neap tide use dotted line graph.*

- *You can see if it spring or neap by looking at the range for the day and compare it with the given mean ranges on the graph.*

FIND TIME FOR A PARTICULAR HEIGHT

Example: *When will the tidal height be 2.5m?*

1. Mark the height of LW on the LW-scale.
2. Mark the height of HW on the HW scale, and draw a line (blue) from point 1 to 2.
7. Enter the height scale at 2.5 m and draw a vertical line down from it.
8. Where this line meets the blue line, draw a horizontal line to the right.
9. Where this line meets the curve for spring tide, draw a vertcal line down to the time scale.
10. Find time to be approx. **4 hrs**. before HW.

- *You can also see if it spring or neap by looking at the moon phase. Springs occur two days after a new or a full moon.*

Electronic navigation

GPS *is now the most prominent navigation system. Decca will be put to rest and Loran will be operative in Europe for another couple of years. Terms such as waypoint, route, cross track error and so on have the same meaning in all system even if the technology differs. Navigation with the help of **Radar** will also be covered along with how it is used to avoid collision with other vessels. We will also look at **digital charts** used in conjunction with a **chart plotter** or a **PC**.*

The GPS antenna *must be unobscured from above in order to receive clear signals from the satellites. It is therefore advisable to mount it on a small mast aft or directly on the pushpit in order to keep it clear of any sails (the top of the mast is not an alternative due to rolling). Make sure it is at least 1m from other antennas and does not get swept by radar.*

1

GPS = Global Positioning System

- ☐ 24 satellites orbit the earth in 6 fixed orbits (4 in each)
- ☐ The orbits are at an altitude of 20 000 km
- ☐ Satellites orbit at a constant rate
- ☐ Each orbit takes about 12 hours

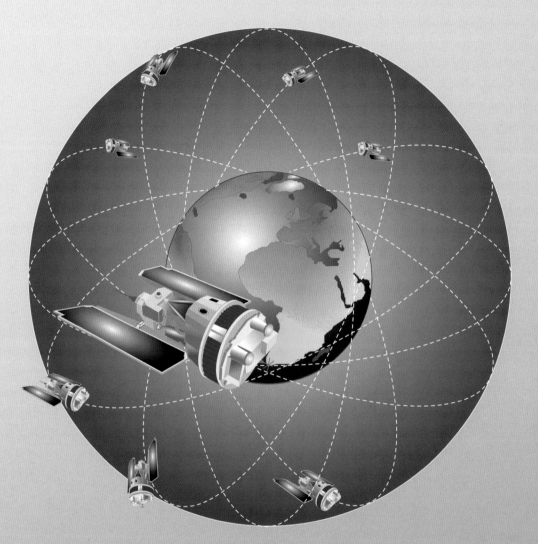

P = ***Precision Code*** is the most accurate code reserved for military use.

C/A = ***Coarse Acquisition*** is the civilian code which is not as accurate but gives a position within 15 m, 95% of the time.

S/A = ***Selective Availability***. The two codes mentioned above were those that were initially sent from the satellites. After a short time it was determined that even the C/A code was ***too accurate***. The Americans added an extra scrambler in order to reduce accuracy even more. The S/A code reduces the accuracy for civilian use to around 100 m, 95% of the time. The US removed this code after a while bringing us at present back to within 15 m, 95% of the time. ***Be aware that the US can add scramblers at any time, even block the system for civilian use if they see fit!***

②

GPS - how does it work?

The 24 satellites orbiting at an altitude of 20 000 km make up a grid surrounding the earth. This makes it possible for your antenna to see at least *the three satellites* required to get a good fix, no matter where you are.

Each satellite informs the GPS of its position and correct time derived from the satellites *hyperaccurate atomic clock*. Based on this the GPS figures out its distance from the satellites resulting in circular *position lines* from each of them. Position lines from two satellites will result in two possible positions as the figure shows. A third satellite produces a new position line which will confirm the position.

Atomic clocks are far too expensive to put in GPS receivers, so the receivers clock will not always show 100% correct time. Therefore the three position lines in the diagram will not intersect in one point. The receiver computes new position lines that will intersect by making minute adjustments to its clock. *This is a very rough explanation of how GPS works.*

The accuracy of the GPS for civilian use is determined by the owners of the system, the US Defence Department. The military P - code gives positions within a meter. All other users awill be subject to "Selective Availability" (p. 38). Here the accuracy is determined by the Pentagon. Russia has their own GPS system and the EU are working on their own which will be compatible with the existing one.

Chart datums

Because the earth does not represent a perfect sphere and because the surface is full of indentations (even at sea), the cartographers have to decide how to describe the earth by choosing a *chart datum* as a reference. There has been some discussion as to where the earth's centre is located (epicentre). The American *WGS-84* (World Geodetic System) is the datum which is being used more and more. You will also encounter ED-50 (European datum) and other datums, especially on older charts.

It is very important that you use the correct chart datum with your GPS. Check on the chart you are using and enter this chart datum in the setup on the GPS. Neglecting this could result in positions being 500 m off. Most charts have a reference to the chart datum used along with a correction based on WGS-84.

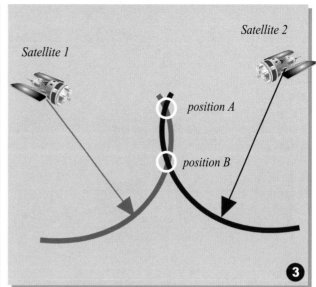

Satellite 1

Satellite 2

position A

position B

3

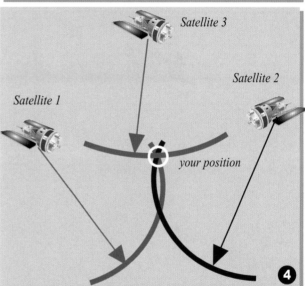

Satellite 3

Satellite 1

Satellite 2

your position

4

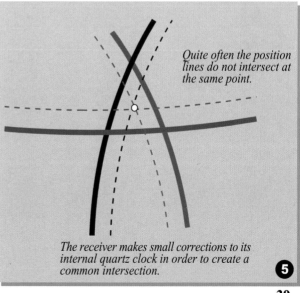

Quite often the position lines do not intersect at the same point.

The receiver makes small corrections to its internal quartz clock in order to create a common intersection.

5

GPS receivers

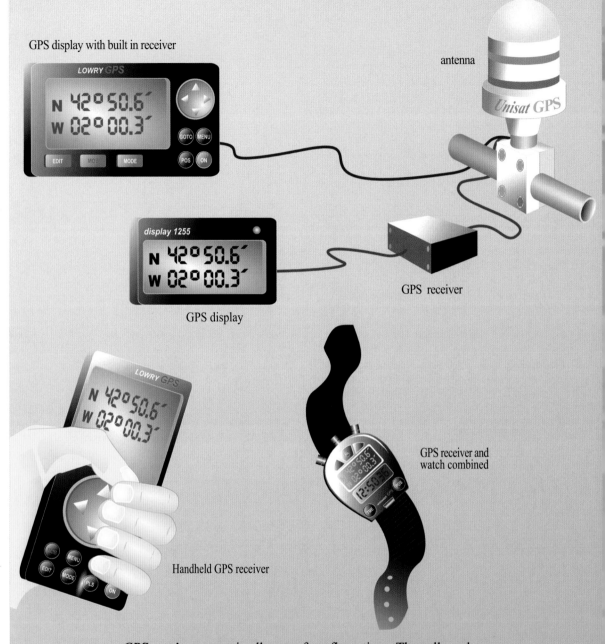

GPS display with built in receiver

antenna

display 1255

GPS display

GPS receiver

Handheld GPS receiver

GPS receiver and watch combined

GPS receivers come in all sorts of configurations. They all need an **antenna**, but many **handheld receivers** have a **built in antenna**. The receiver itself can be a "black box" which has to be hooked up to a **display** (small screen) or a **PC**. A proper antenna mounted outside (on the pushpit for example) is important in order to have a reliable system if the receiver is used below decks, where a built in antenna would not function properly.

6

Using the GPS receiver

The easiest way to use a GPS receiver is to read off the position (1) and mark it off on the chart. Be as accurate as possible. Note that *minutes* are with *decimals* as in this example: 18.5'. The charts usually divide each minute into ten. If a minute is referred to with *two* decimals you have to approximate it. Keep in mind that 1/100 of a minute represents 18.5 m. Rounding off won't cause much of an error.

Waypoint

A waypoint can be *any point* you want to use as a reference. It can be a buoy where you started your trip, or any point you want to pass through on your way, or the entrance to the harbour at your destination.

The GPS receiver is capable of storing a large number of waypoints. You can give them any name you want, omitting this they will be designated WP1, WP2, WP3 and so on. You have to enter *Lat* and *Long* for every waypoint. *Be accurate in order to avoid errors which could have serious consequences!*

Example: 1. You are in pos. A on p. 25 (59°18.5'N, 013° 32.5'E) and wish to proceed to pos. B. Enter B as a waypoint and call it **WPB**.

N.B. Because each make of GPS has different setup menus and layouts, we refer to a general procedure here. Refer to the manual for your particular unit for more details.

At any time you can define a waypoint and choose GO TO WAYPOINT from the menu and read out *true bearing* BRG and *distance* DIST to that WP (5). You can also see *course* and *speed over ground* (COG and SOG) which indicates how the passage is progressing.

N.B. Course Over Ground (COG) is the same as Track or Track over Ground used earlier in the book. The term track is used in electronic navigation as the track over ground you actually have travelled.
You may also in some books or manuals see the terms Course Made Good (CMG) which is the same as COG and Speed Made Good (SMG) which is the same as Speed Over Ground, SOG.

- ☐ **BRG** = Bearing to waypoint
- ☐ **XTE** = Cross Track Error (off set from course line)
- ☐ **DIST** = Distance to waypoint
- ☐ **COG** = Course Over Ground = Track
- ☐ **SOG** = Speed Over Ground
- ☐ **DTG** = Distance to go = DIST= distance to WP

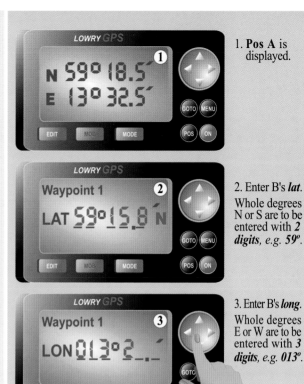

1. **Pos A** is displayed.

2. Enter B's *lat*. Whole degrees N or S are to be entered with *2 digits*, e.g. *59°*.

3. Enter B's *long*. Whole degrees E or W are to be entered with *3 digits*, e.g. *013°*.

4. *Save* the WP with name of your choice.

7

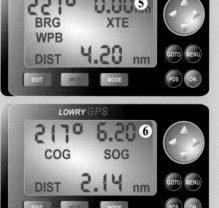

5. TB (**BRG**) to WP is 227° and the distance (**DIST**) is 4.2 M.

6. Halfway to WP B we have:
COG = 217°
SOG = 6.2 kn.
DIST= 2.14 M.

N.B.: nm = M = nautical mile

8

7. If we refer to the display we had earlier (5) the BRG has changed to 238° and XTE has changed from 0.00 to 0.41 M. We see that we have wandered 0.41 M off the course line to port due to wind, current or poor steering.

⌐ = Turn to **port**
⌐ = Turn to **stbd**.

When you see that your COG differs from BRG you usually make a course adjustment to compensate for current or tide. Most newer receivers have a graphic display showing your position relative to your course line. Otherwise XTE will be displayed with symbols similar to those shown above.

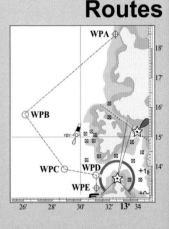

Course line = 227°
Distance = 4.2 M
COG = 217°
new BRG = 238°
XTE=0.41 M
10°

Here we see that wind and current has set us 10° off course and put us 0.41 M from our course line. The new BRG is now 238° but you know that you have to steer another 10° to stbd in order to compensate for wind and current, resulting in 248°T. **9**

As you start to sail towards a WP keep an eye on **COG** and **XTE** to correct your track towards your goal. If you at the same time compare **SOG** with your log, you can get a picture of what wind and current are doing. In the example you have gone halfway to the waypoint and note that leeway is 10°. But as you are already 0.41 M off the course line you have to steer 238° + 10° = 248°T in order to keep a correct COG.

Routes

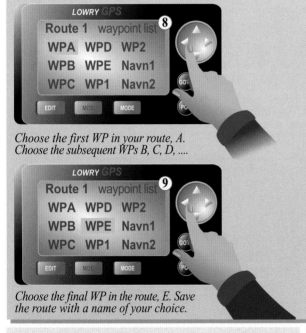

Choose the first WP in your route, A. Choose the subsequent WPs B, C, D, ...

Choose the final WP in the route, E. Save the route with a name of your choice.

N.B. All the WPs are stored in a **WP list**. They can be picked from here in any order you choose in order to make up a **route. You should always plot all the waypoints on a chart to ensure that the route is safe! (When using a chart plotter you may have to zoom in and out and pan along the route.)**

10

Route: If you enter the points A, B, C, D and E on p. 25 as WPs in the WP list before your passage, you can create *a route* using the ROUTE function. The unit will ask you to define WPs for this route, from start to finish. The route can then be saved with the name of your choice. When starting off you define this *saved* route as your active route. The GPS unit will show you BRG and DIST to the first WP in the route. When you arrive at the WP the unit will change to the next WP, showing BRG and DIST to that one. Certain units let you specify proximity range for changing to next or sound an alarm. *N.B. This differs between GPS receivers.*

Chart plotters

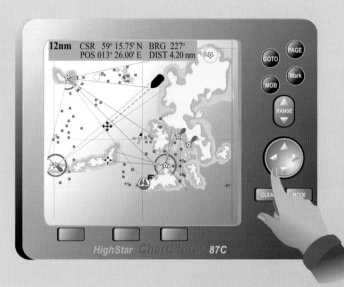

A PC can be hooked up to a GPS receiver and other instruments via a serial cable and a software package. The possibilities are endless. The biggest problem could prove to be the navigators dwindling ability to navigate using traditional methods!

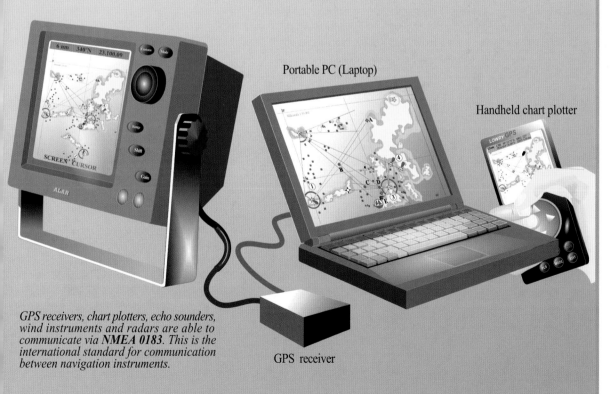

Portable PC (Laptop)

Handheld chart plotter

GPS receivers, chart plotters, echo sounders, wind instruments and radars are able to communicate via **NMEA 0183**. This is the international standard for communication between navigation instruments.

GPS receiver

11

Using the chart plotter

When you turn on the chart plotter the chart will appear. You can *zoom in* and out using the *range button*. You will get a warning if there are no chart details for your area. *We refer to one certain chart plotter which may differ from yours, but the main principles should be similar.*

If you wish to *centre* the chart, push FIND SHIP button. You will find yourself in the centre of the chart marked with a boat symbol. As you sail along, the symbol will move towards the edge of the chart. You can re-centre it by pushing FIND SHIP, HOME or CENTER, depending on your unit. *Many units will keep the vessel in the centre while the chart moves.*

Along the top of the screen you will see your POS along with other information like COG and DIST.

If you move the cursor the information on the top will now change from the *vessel position* VES POS to *cursor position* CRS POS on the unit shown here. *The cursor* can have many shapes, shown here as a cross. The *cursor control* can be a ball, buttons or a mouse. *Get the feel of whichever one you have!*

Electronic charts come in two major categories:

Raster charts are "pictures" of the original paper charts. These are *scanned in* as millions of colour points (pixels) and reproduced on your screen using a software program. This is the easiest, quickest and cheapest way to make an electronic chart. Some producers are NOAA (USA), ARCS (UK) and BSB charts from Maptech.

The drawback with raster charts is that all information is contained within the same layer and is difficult to edit or update. If you attempt to zoom in, the chart will only appear larger without giving more detail. You have no control over what information to display. A raster chart takes up a lot of space on the storage medium. This also means slower downloads and updates.

Vector charts are recognized by most plotters. These charts are made from scratch using short line segments (vectors) of different shapes from available chart data. All this is stored in different *layers* which you can display by choice. The vector charts (represented by Navionics and C-MAP amongst others) are more expensive than raster charts but give more control over how to display information, giving you better focus on important details concerning your passage.

Centering the chart

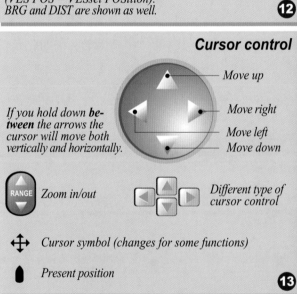

If you press the button under FIND SHIP (also HOME among others) the chart will orient itself with the vessel in the centre. Note that the vessel's position is shown at the top of the screen (VES POS = VESsel POSition). BRG and DIST are shown as well.

12

Cursor control

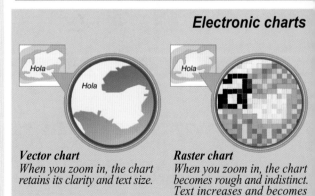

If you hold down be-tween the arrows the cursor will move both vertically and horizontally.

Move up
Move right
Move left
Move down

RANGE *Zoom in/out*

Different type of cursor control

Cursor symbol (changes for some functions)

Present position

13

Electronic charts

Hola
Hola

Hola

Vector chart
When you zoom in, the chart retains its clarity and text size.

Raster chart
When you zoom in, the chart becomes rough and indistinct. Text increases and becomes indiscernible as you zoom in.

14

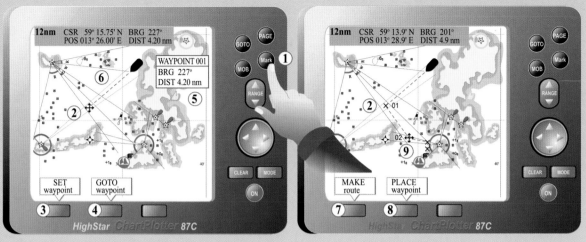

When choosing the **WP function** (1) you must move the cursor to the new WP position (2) as shown on the diagram. Press the button marked SET waypoint (3). **N.B. Different plotters have different ways of doing this.**

When choosing **route function** (7) move the cursor to the first WP in your route (2) and press PLACE waypoint (8). Move the cursor to the next WP (9) and repeat the procedure. **15**

You can create WPs with the cursor. You can go to the WP (4) or just store it in WP list. If you choose GOTO waypoint the display will show BRG and DIST on the screen (5) and a line will indicate your course line (a red broken line) to WP (6).

The **Route** function allows you to create a route with cursor control. Place the cursor where you want the different WPs and **acknowledge** by pressing a button. These buttons are often unmarked as they are designated on the screen, so called "**soft keys**".

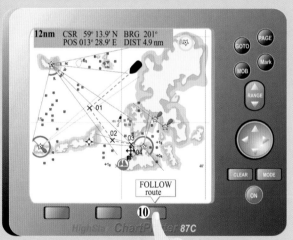

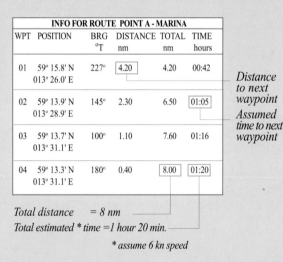

INFO FOR ROUTE POINT A - MARINA				
WPT	POSITION	BRG °T	DISTANCE nm	TOTAL nm	TIME hours
01	59° 15.8' N 013° 26.0' E	227°	4.20	4.20	00:42
02	59° 13.9' N 013° 28.9' E	145°	2.30	6.50	01:05
03	59° 13.7' N 013° 31.1' E	100°	1.10	7.60	01:16
04	59° 13.3' N 013° 31.1' E	180°	0.40	8.00	01:20

Distance to next waypoint

Assumed time to next waypoint

Total distance = 8 nm

Total estimated * time =1 hour 20 min.

* assume 6 kn speed

Continue until you have chosen FOLLOW route (10) and you the first WP. Note that the plotter with numbers 01, 02, 03 and so forth write that with names of your own).

the last WP. Press are ready to go to designates the WPs (you may over-

16

It is important to keep in mind that we are only explaining the principles and examples of functions and names. Study the manual for your designated plotter! When you have chosen all the waypoints you can save the route under a *name of your choice* for easy recognition. You can do this with the waypoints as well. Use names you will recognize. When you have

created a route you can display information about the route on the screen including DIST, BRG and time between WPs along with total DIST and time from start to finish. This is very useful in order to check that everything is correct. *It is important to use your knowledge of navigation along with common sense to double-check the information displayed by the plotter.*

Track

The *track* will give an indication of how the boat has sailed compared to the course line. This is very useful, especially with wind and current present. You can turn it on or off and even save it for later reference.

Split screen

Most plotters give you the ability to split the screen, enabling you to view the radar and chart at the same time. Choosing NORTH-UP on the radar, as described in the radar section, makes it easier to compare the two.

Radar/chart overlay

Some plotters allow you to lay the radar image on top of the chart imposing radar echoes right on the chart along with your position.

Defining chart UP

Chart plotters usually enable you to choose how the chart is displayed. If you choose HEADING-UP your track will at all times point straight up. The chart moves towards you from the top of the screen which makes it easier to compare the chart to what you see around you.

N.B. Be aware when setting up the chart this way as it makes it difficult to determine distances and bearings as the chart is always moving.

It is recommended to choose NORTH-UP when displaying radar and chart together on the screen.

Log-data

Plotters can be programmed to save passage data at set intervals, for example every half hour.

Information windows

Most plotters are able to display information windows based on choices defined by the user.

We have shown some of the possible functions on modern chart plotters. New models with added functionality are appearing all the time, but the basics are more or less the same.

 MOB (Man OverBoard) *If this button is pressed a waypoint with a designated symbol is created. Distance and bearing to this point are displayed continuously.*

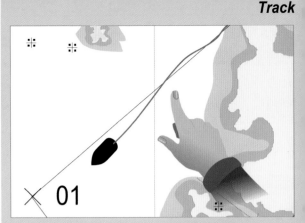

*The **track** shows you how you are actually moving over ground. This is very useful, especially with wind and current present.* **17**

Split screen

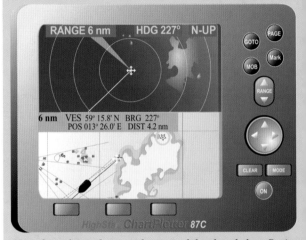

Here the radar is shown at the top and the chart below. Setting the radar NORTH-UP (p.55) helps comparison.

Radar overlay

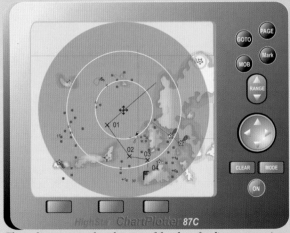

The radar image is placed on top of the chart for direct comparison. **18**

General aspects of how to set up your GPS receiver or Chart-plotter (common term *navigator*) correctly.

Once again we recommend you to refer to the manual for your particular unit.

A list of buttons you will most likely encounter:

☐ **ON/OFF** - turns the navigator on and off. Depress for a couple of seconds to activate.

☐ **NAV** - initiates or ends navigation with way-points or routes.

☐ **MOB** - (Man Over Board) - used to mark a point of importance. A waypoint is created and the display shows BRG and DIST to this point.

☐ **ZOOM** - used to "zoom" in and out of the chart. Same function as the RANGE button in this book.

☐ **PAGE** - used to move through pages of import-ant information. Also used to end an operation and return to the main page.

☐ **MENU** - used to display a menu page referring to the relevant main page.

☐ **ENTER** - can have several functions. Activate a data field for entering data or verifying an action.

☐ **SETUP** - is used to enter units, formats, chart datums and other parameters in the navigator.

It is *very important* to achieve a correct setup of the navigator. This plays a vital role in how position and other information are presented. *This is one area you shouldn't experiment with*. Pushing buttons can otherwise be a good way to explore your unit's capabilities.

Try to avoid this method in setup however, as this controls how the navigator interprets charts and how information is displayed. Before setting off on a passage make sure the information in setup is correct.

Let's look at some examples of settings in setup:

☐ **Language:**		english
☐ **Date format:**		dd/mm/yy
☐ **Time**		24 hours
☐ **Time zone**		+1
☐ **Height**		meter*
☐ **Speed unit**		knots
☐ **Distance units**		nautical mile
☐ **Chart datum**		WGS 84

Chart datum is the most important setting. Chart plotters get this information automatically from the digital charts they use. For stand alone receivers it should be set according to the information in every chart that is being used. Check the chart datum in the setup menu every time you go from one chart to another.

* UTC offset +1 indicates that the time shown is one hour ahead of UTC (Zone +1).

** The GPS will also calculate your elevation. This is not too interesting at sea!

It is absolutely necessary to emphasize that the cartography is not always accurate. You should check the source diagram on paper charts to see when they were surveyed and at what scale. Quite a few charts both in the UK and elsewhere were surveyed in 19th century using a lead line and compass! Errors of several miles may occur!

Chart plotters can be dangerous to use if these errors are not understood! It is utterly important to use all your traditional navigation skills to check your chartplotter all the time.

Own notes

RADAR
(RAdio Direction And Range)

The radar appears at the top of many navigators "best equipment" list because it is able to "see" land and other vessels in fog and darkness, giving BRG and DIST to marks and lighthouses as well.

The price of a recreational radar has come down to a level which allows more and more to mount one on board their boat. They have become more compact and even the "cheap" ones do a pretty good job.

The radar consists of transmitter, receiver, control unit and **antenna**. The first three are usually incorporated with the screen. The antenna is mounted high and unobscured and rotates at 15 - 35 rpm driven by an electric motor.

The antenna transmits radio pulses and receives the echoes a split second later. The pulses stream out at a great rate in all directions, and by calculating the time delay of the echoes, **the range** and **distance** to **the object** (e.g. a ship) causing the echo, can be found.

The radar screen is usually combined with the transmitter, receiver and control unit. Initially the screens were CRT, like TV screens, but now they are usually digital LCD screens, as also TVs and and PC monitors are becoming. These screens use less power and are easier to view in daylight.

The radar sends and receives short high frequency radio pulses with wavelengths between 3 and 10 cm (we refer to them as "3 cm radar or 10 cm radar").

3 cm = X band, around 10 GHz
10 cm = S-band, around   3 GHz.

The antenna should be mounted high up and have unobscured sight. Masts and superstructure can produce a "shadow" or "false" echo. In leisure craft 4 m is considered a good height. This antenna is mounted inside a **radome** (plastic housing).

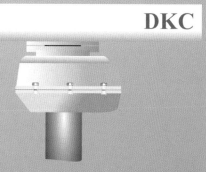

Echoes from ships, buoys and land appears as lit "lumps".

Larger antennas (with a narrower horizontal beam width) are open and rotate on their drive shaft.

The cheapest small craft radars have a transmitting power of 1 to 2 kW. This usually means a range of about 16 to 24 M. Larger radars transmitting at 4 kW have a range of up to 36 M.

19

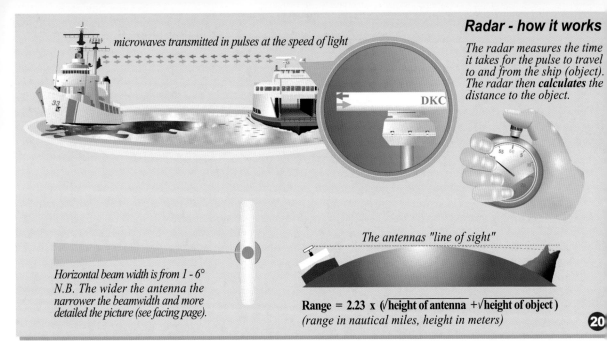

Radar - how it works

microwaves transmitted in pulses at the speed of light

DKC

The radar measures the time it takes for the pulse to travel to and from the ship (object). The radar then **calculates** the distance to the object.

Horizontal beam width is from 1 - 6°
N.B. The wider the antenna the narrower the beamwidth and more detailed the picture (see facing page).

The antennas "line of sight"

Range = 2.23 x ($\sqrt{\text{height of antenna}}$ + $\sqrt{\text{height of object}}$)
(range in nautical miles, height in meters)

20

Pulses are transmitted from the antenna at the speed of light (300 000 km/sec or 162 000 nm/sec). This is so fast that the antenna has hardly moved by the time the pulse returns. The antenna rotates at a constant speed so the radar knows at what angle to its axis the pulse was transmitted or the reflected pulse received (same angle). The radar is able to calculate **both distance and bearing to the object.**

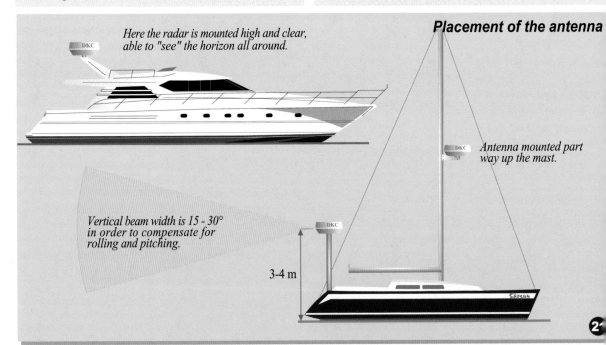

Placement of the antenna

Here the radar is mounted high and clear, able to "see" the horizon all around.

DKC

Antenna mounted part way up the mast.

Vertical beam width is 15 - 30° in order to compensate for rolling and pitching.

DKC

3-4 m

DKC

Shazam

2'

Theoretically **the antenna** should be mounted as high as possible in order to "see" as far as possible. But if it's mounted too high pitching and heeling will reduce its "vision". Added weight should be kept low as well. 3 - 4 meters above sea level is the norm on pleasure crafts. Keep at least 2 m away from the **antenna in order to avoid being fried by the sweep!**

The radar's range depends more on line of sight than the wattage. The radar can "see" a little further than the straight line due to refraction of the microwaves (slightly more than light) in the atmosphere. The range is often limited to 10 to15 M due to line of sight, even if the producers might claim it to be 24 M

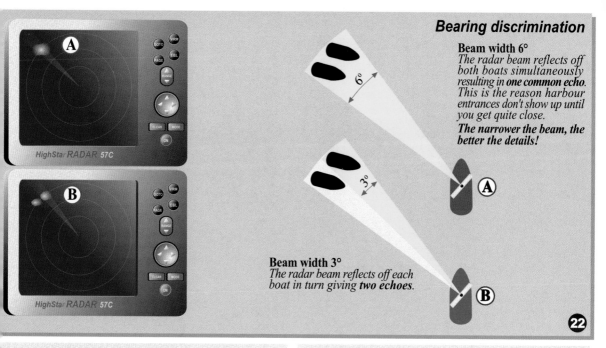

Bearing discrimination

Beam width 6°
*The radar beam reflects off both boats simultaneously resulting in **one common echo**. This is the reason harbour entrances don't show up until you get quite close.*

The narrower the beam, the better the details!

Beam width 3°
*The radar beam reflects off each boat in turn giving **two echoes**.*

22

Horizontal beam width is important for the radar's ability to distinguish between objects close together. With a 6° beam width the radar beam from boat A would reflect off the two black boats at the same time, giving one echo. Boat B transmits a 3° beam. A pulse reaches the first boat and produces an echo. The next pulse bounces off the other boat giving a *new echo* separate from the first.

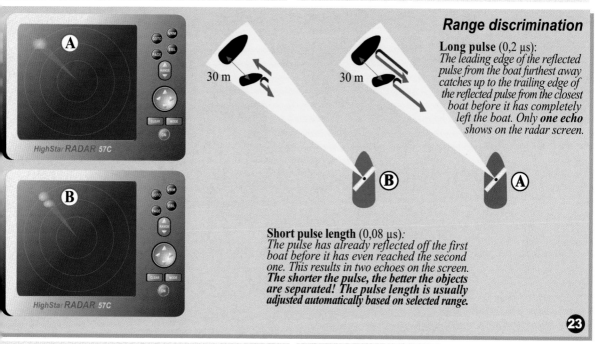

Range discrimination

Long pulse (0,2 µs):
*The leading edge of the reflected pulse from the boat furthest away catches up to the trailing edge of the reflected pulse from the closest boat before it has completely left the boat. Only **one echo** shows on the radar screen.*

30 m

30 m

Short pulse length (0,08 µs):
The pulse has already reflected off the first boat before it has even reached the second one. This results in two echoes on the screen.
The shorter the pulse, the better the objects are separated! The pulse length is usually adjusted automatically based on selected range.

23

The pulse length (defined in µs = microseconds) is crucial to the radars ability to distinguish two objects in line with each other. The radar on boat A has a pulse length of 0.2 µs. The radar beam travels 60 m in the course of the life-span of the pulse. If the two boats are within 30 m of each other, the "same" pulse will reflect off the furthest target and return to and catch up to the trailing edge of the reflected pulse off the closest target. The radar will read this as *one echo*. Boat B transmits a pulse of 0.08 µs (travels 24 m). The tail end of the reflected pulse from the first boat will be in front of the the leading edge of the reflected pulse from the one furthest away. The radar detects *two echoes*.

Radar operation

After turning the radar on with the ***power on/off*** button, it takes 1 - 3 minutes before it's ready to use. It will first go into STANDBY mode where everything is ready to go but pulses are not being transmitted. When you finally press TRANSMIT (= TX) the antenna will start rotating and the radar will send and receive pulses. N.B. Some radars require you to press ***power*** or some other button. At this point it is important to adjust the radar (many radars do this more or less automatically).

☐ **BRILLIANCE** is adjusted to a level you prefer.

☐ **GAIN** is important to adjust correctly. This is the amplification of the received echoes. If it's too low, echoes from small objects may be omitted. If it's too high, the screen will show lots of small dots which could obscure small echoes. Best setting is when these dots are barely visible.

☐ **RANGE** determines how far the radar "sees", from close up ($^1/_8$ M - $^1/_4$ M = 230 - 460 meters) up to $^1/_2$, 1, 2, 3, 6, 8 and 24 M on a typical small craft vessel. Initially you start adjusting the radar at a range of 3 - 6 M. Define a target in the chosen range for tuning purposes.

☐ **TUNING** is crucial in the quality of the reception of echoes from surrounding objects. As a rule you have correct tuning when the picture is sharpest. Some radars have indicators (fig.24) to assist tuning. The procedure should be carried out every time you change range, but help is at hand:

☐ **AUTOMATIC TUNING**, found on many radars, will do the job for you every time you turn on the radar or change the range.

☐ **SEA CLUTTER** can be a problem. Because of the large ***vertical beam width*** (usually 25 - 30°), it is possible that the waves close to the boat reflect signals, especially if the boat is rolling or pitching. ***Use this adjustment with care!*** Too much damping can erase echoes from objects.

☐ **RAIN CLUTTER** isn't as demanding as the adjustment above. The water in a rain shower reflects the signals differently from a dense wave. A rain shower will show up more "fluffy" than a dense object. ***The radar can be used to avoid rain squalls during unstable weather!***

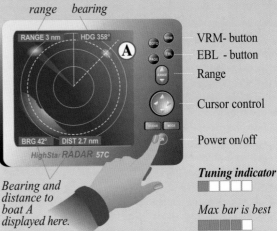

range   bearing

VRM- button
EBL - button
Range

Cursor control

Power on/off

Bearing and distance to boat A displayed here.

Tuning indicator

Max bar is best

*The radar is adjusted and chosen range is 3 M. **Range rings** show the distance from the centre (your position) in equal increments (here 1 M). The rings make it easier to visualize the distance of objects in your vicinity.*

*If you require the accurate range and bearing to boat A, you choose the **VRM** function (Variable Range Marker) and adjust a circle (broken line) with the **cursor control** until it intersects the target. A distance of 2.7 M is displayed. Choose the **EBL** (Electronic Bearing Line) function and draw the broken line through the target with the cursor control. You will get a **relative bearing** displayed (in this case 42°). You can display **true bearing** if the radar receives heading information from other instruments. **N.B. Buttons and menus differ on various makes of radar even though the principles are similar.***

24

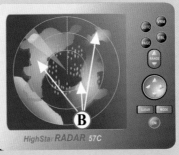

Echoes from rain showers (B) appear larger and more drawn out than solid objects. The edges are rougher and on some displays they have a blue/red hue

25

GAIN

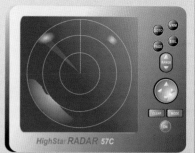

Too much Gain: "Snow" in the display hides the weak echo A.

Correct Gain: Trace of snow but weak echo A is visible.

Not enough Gain: Snow is gone but so is weak echo A.

TUNE

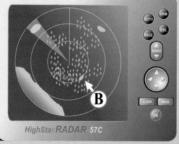

Incorrect Tune: No echo

Correct Tune: Visible echoes with good contrast.

Poor Tune: Some echoes not visible, others are fuzzy.

SEA CLUTTER (use with caution!)

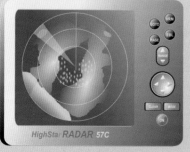
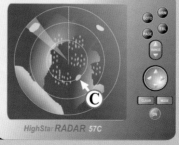

Not enough Sea Clutter: A lot of "snow" surrounding own vessel hides echo B.

Correct Sea Clutter: Some snow but weak echo B is visible.

Too much Sea Clutter: Almost all snow gone but so is echo B.

RAIN CLUTTER (use with caution!)

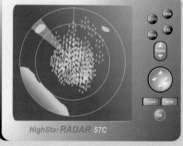

Not enough RAIN Clutter: A lot of "snow" caused by rain/squalls.

Correct Rain Clutter: You see the rain shower and echo C is visible.

Too much Rain Clutter: All "snow" from rain shower is gone, along with the echo.

26

Problems encountered with radar display

In order to utilize the radar properly it's imperative that you learn how to *interpret* the information displayed. Many objects produce such a poor echo that they don't show up on the screen. Wooden as well as fiberglass boats can give a poor echo. Anyone who has been on the bridge of a large vessel is aware that small boats often don't show up on the radar screen. *Always assume that you won't be seen by other vessels and act accordingly.*

Both fixed and floating markers and buoys usually show up quite well. *Radar shadows* and indistinguishable echoes (see next page) is a problem as well. Keep in mind that the coastline and configurations of islands may appear totally different compared to the chart and elevated land masses inland are often visible before the coastline. *Only practical experience can teach you to interpret the radar display correctly!*

Blind spots due to mast and superstructure can also be a problem. *False echoes* can often occur in conjunction with blind spots as shown in the fig. Here it's the mast which causes a false echo. The radar pulse reflects off the mast and if it hits a target it will reflect back the same way.

The false echo (E) will appear in the direction of the mast with a distance equal to the "true" target (D).

In addition, *interference* from other radars can disturb the display as well. *Therefore take every opportunity to practise interpreting what you see on the display. In daylight and clear weather, compare what you see with your own eyes to the display, while referring it all to the chart.*

The radar's minimum distance: Every time a pulse is transmitted the receiver is blocked in order to avoid receiving an echo before the pulse is completed. That is why the pulses are short at close range. Usually the minimum distance will be slightly greater than its range discrimination ability, around 20 -30 m.

Navigating with radar

A *Racon* (RAdar beaCON) makes it possible to identify specific lights or markers. It transmits signals in *morse code* a split second after its *echo returns* to your radar. The beacon is located where the morse signal originates.

The Racon signal is transmitted only after every third or fourth sweep of your radar. This is to preserve energy and avoid cluttering your display with the morse signals.

The examples shown here are typical of how you navigate with radar. Keep in mind that a wide horizontal beam width (4 - 6°) can result in equivalent discrepancies in bearing. Distance is much more accurate.

Radar shadow

You won't be able to see the bay on your screen until you have sailed a bit further.

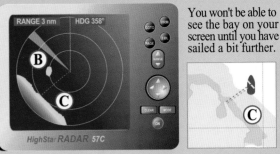

Boat A won't show up as the radar beam is unable to "see" through boat B. Only one echo appears on the screen.

False echo

mast

A curved mast can reflect the radar pulse causing it to bounce off boat D producing a false echo.

In addition to the real echo from boat D it produces a false echo in the direction of the mast E.

27

Racon

Katten transmits a Racon beacon N in morse code —•

True bearing to Katten is 81° and distance is 1.8 M. True heading is 303°. N.B. If the radar receives heading from a fluxgate compass, for example, the radar can display true bearings (bearing followed by a T). If no such information is available the bearing is relative. In this case it is 138°.

If cardinal markers are equipped with Racon they would transmit morse code referring to their directions:

N = North: —•   S = South:•••   E = East: •   W = West: •—•

28

Display setup

Most radars for pleasure craft are set up so that the boat is in the *centre* and the white *heading marker* points *up*. Everything on the right side of the screen is found on your starboard side and everything on the left side of the screen is found on your port side. Things that appear on the lower half of the screen are behind you.

This setup is called **HEAD-UP** because your heading is always up on the screen. The radar picture moves down the screen as the boat moves forward, turning as the boat turns. This is called *an unstabilized image*. The advantage with this setup is that it is easier to interpret for new users. If the helmsman (or autopilot) is unable to keep a steady course, taking bearings and distances can be a problem.

As you become a little more experienced it is advisable to set up a *stabilized image* as used on larger vessels. This setup is called **NORTH-UP**. The radar must then receive heading information from a *gyro* or a *fluxgate compass*. This has the following advantages:

☐ The radar picture has the same orientation as the chart, making it easier to compare what you see.

☐ The echoes are stationary. Even if the helmsman weaves about, the image is *stabilized*.
☐ You get an immediate indication of changes in heading.

COURSE-UP uses the course line in a route to stabilize the picture when navigating from WP to WP. The active leg points up.

Large radars on large vessels are often set to **TRUE MOTION**. All land and fixed markers are static, while echoes from other vessels and your own boat move around on the screen. This might seem optimal but has some restrictions.

Collision avoidance

A classic rule is that if the bearing to a converging vessel is *constant over time*, the two vessels are on a *collision course*. It doesn't matter if you use true, magnetic or compass bearing or refer to fixed marks on board. On the next page we will look at how to use this principle with radar.

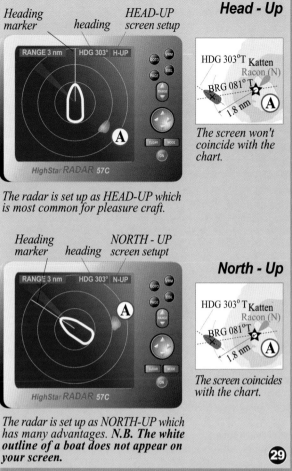

The radar is set up as HEAD-UP which is most common for pleasure craft.

The screen won't coincide with the chart.

*The radar is set up as NORTH-UP which has many advantages. **N.B. The white outline of a boat does not appear on your screen.***

The screen coincides with the chart.

29

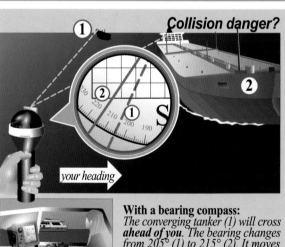

Collision danger?

With a bearing compass:
*The converging tanker (1) will cross **ahead of you**. The bearing changes from 205° (1) to 215° (2). It moves forward.*

Using fixed marks:
*(frame in windscreen) The woman on board observes that the other vessel moves astern in the window frame, from 3 - 4. Her boat will clear ahead (4) if both boats maintain speed and heading because the bearing changes further **astern**.*

30

You define an echo 42° relative on your starboard bow (1), distance 3 M and another 45° on your port bow (4), same distance.

*6 min. later the first boat is closer but with the **same bearing** (2). This indicates a **collision course**. The other boat is abeam to port and much closer (5) but seems to go clear.*

*Another 6 min. later and the first boat is only 1 M away with the same bearing (3). **You must take action to avoid collision!** (See the collision regulations, COLREGs). The other boat (6) will go astern of you and doesn't represent any danger.*

31

Judging speed and direction of other boats on the screen is difficult because it shows everything as *relative motion* to your boat and your speed is not known (except in TRUE MOTION). You observe that an echo moves from 1 to 2 to 3, but judging speed and true heading is impossible. *Radar plotting* will give you a picture of what is happening (see below).

Radar plotting/ ARPA

Assumed boat speed = 5 knts   Head Up   *RadarPlot*

CPA = 0 = Collision!

CPA = 1 M $0.7 \times 10 = 7$ kts

$1.9 \times 10 = 19$ kts

The plot sheet is a compass rose with distance rings in nm. If you plot every 6 min. = 1/10 hour, all you have to do is multiply by ten in order to find your speed in knots.

1. Find and mark on plot sheet the distance and bearing (use VRM and EBL) to boat in position (1) and (2) and draw the line 1-2.
2. Draw your speed (5kts in this case) from 1 to A (always vertical).
3. Draw the line from A to 2. That is the other boat's track. Measure A-2 and multiply by 10. You then have the other boat's speed.

Use this procedure to find the second boat's track and speed (pos 4 & 5). Repeat for 2 & 3 and 5 & 6. The broken lines extending 1 & 2 and 4&5 show how the other boats will approach you. (CPA = Closest Point of Approach, 0 and 1 M in each case).

ARPA is active and you get relative speed and track for the two boats (7 & 8). You see that one of the boats is on a collision course while the other will go clear astern.

The line shows track and the length shows speed.

NB! Small boats use the cheaper system MARPA, not ARPA.   **32**

The radar plot gives you the *true speed and track* of the vessels you plot. Relative track and speed (green) combined with own track and speed (blue) results in what is illustrated (similar to vectors in tidal streams and currents). Use time intervals of 6 or 12 min. as this equals to 1/10 and 1/5 of an hour. This makes it easier to avoid making mistakes. Large radars on larger ships are often able to show *true* track and speed of targets (ARPA = Automatic Radar Plotting). *Don't have blind faith in electronics and especially ARPA. The radar could be set up wrongly or not working properly. Your interpretation could be incorrect. Be observant and use all you know about navigation and verify the information from the radar!*

Own notes

CELESTIAL NAVIGATION

Celestial navigation allows you to find your position using a sextant, watch, nautical almanac and tables. You measure the height of the sun or another heavenly body while making a note of the exact time. With the help of an almanac, tables and a little figuring, you can find your position.

Contrary to electronic navigational equipment like GPS, celestial navigation is not reliant on electricity. On long ocean passages it's a good idea to bring along the tools of this trade.

The sun's GP

The sun seems to be moving around the earth every 24 hrs. At any given time the sun is right overhead somewhere on the earth - the sun is in **Zenith**. Areas where the sun *can* be in Zenith are between N 23½° and S 23½°. These circles of latitude are called the **Tropic of Cancer** and the **Tropic of Capricorn**.

The point where an imaginary line from the centre of the sun to the centre of the earth intersects the earths surface is called the **sun's GP** (Geographic Position). GPs always move towards the west and take 24 hrs per revolution and its angle west of the Greenwich meridian is called **GHA** (Greenwich hour angle). It moves slowly north or south depending on the time of year and it's angle N or S of the equator is called **declination**.

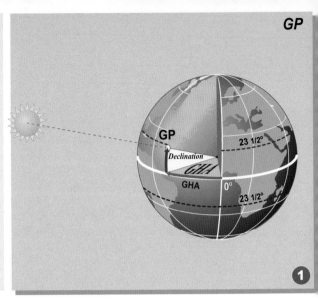

1

The Ecliptic

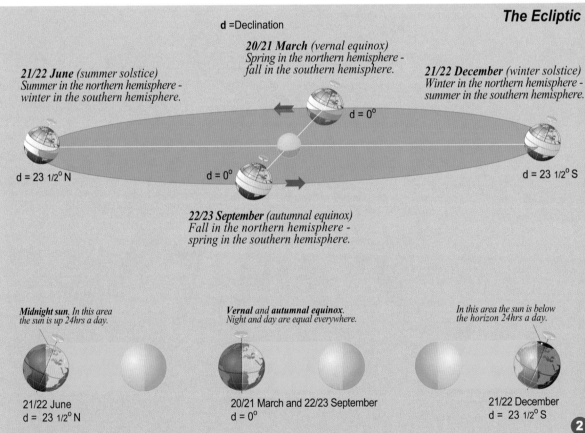

d =Declination

20/21 March *(vernal equinox)*
Spring in the northern hemisphere -
fall in the southern hemisphere.

21/22 June *(summer solstice)*
Summer in the northern hemisphere -
winter in the southern hemisphere.

21/22 December *(winter solstice)*
Winter in the northern hemisphere -
summer in the southern hemisphere.

d = 0°

d = 23 1/2° N

d = 0°

d = 23 1/2° S

22/23 September *(autumnal equinox)*
Fall in the northern hemisphere -
spring in the southern hemisphere.

Midnight sun. *In this area the sun is up 24hrs a day.*

Vernal and **autumnal equinox.** *Night and day are equal everywhere.*

In this area the sun is below the horizon 24hrs a day.

21/22 June
d = 23 1/2° N

20/21 March and 22/23 September
d = 0°

21/22 December
d = 23 1/2° S

2

The earth orbits the sun once every year. The earth's orbital plane, **the ecliptic**, is at an angle of about 23° with the equator. This explains the seasons as shown above. When the tilt of the earth's axis points towards the sun, we experience summer in the northern hemisphere - with longer days and the sun higher in the sky. During the winter (and the Southern hemisphere) the situation is opposite.

The declination is maximum 23½° summer and winter. At the **vernal** and **autumnal** equinox, night and day are equal everywhere on the planet. The declination is then 0°.

Midnight sun and winter darkness is also due to the ecliptic and occurs summer and winter in both hemispheres.

Astronomical model

The earth orbits the sun and all the while it rotates around its own axis every 24 hrs. In celestial navigation we assume that the earth is a *static central point* in an enormous sphere, known as the *celestial sphere*, onto which we consider the sun, moon, planets and stars to be placed. This sphere rotates around us every 24hrs.

The stars are considered to be fixed while the sun, moon and planets constantly change positions in relation to each other as well as the stars.

As the radius of the earth is very small compared to the radius of the celestial sphere, we assume that the observer's eye is located at the centre of the earth. The equator, circles of latitude, meridians and positions are projected out on the sphere.

This inaccurate model enables us to navigate using celestial bodies even if our calculations are not 100 percent accurate. With table corrections we achieve sufficient accuracy from our sextant observations which measure the altitudes of heavenly bodies.

Altitude

The altitude of a celestial body is its angle above the horizon, in degrees, usually measured with a sextant. Even if we focus primarily on navigation using the sun in this book, the majority of the principles can be used with other celestial bodies mentioned at the end of the book.

Azimuth

Azimuth angle on the northern hemisphere is the angle along the horizon from true north to a vertical line through the celestial body. On the southern hemisphere it is the angle along the horizon from true south to a vertical line through the celestial body. In other words, Azimuth angle is the shortest way to the vertical through the body from either due north or south.

It is the Azimuth angle (Z) which is found in the tables. You have to change this to true bearing on the chart, *Azimuth (Zn)*. In the tables in fig. 18 there is an explanation on how to convert Z to Zn in different situations. If you are in doubt about your calculations, double-check with a compass bearing.

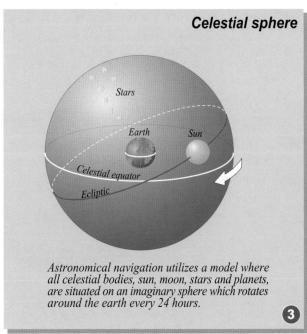

Celestial sphere

Astronomical navigation utilizes a model where all celestial bodies, sun, moon, stars and planets, are situated on an imaginary sphere which rotates around the earth every 24 hours.

3

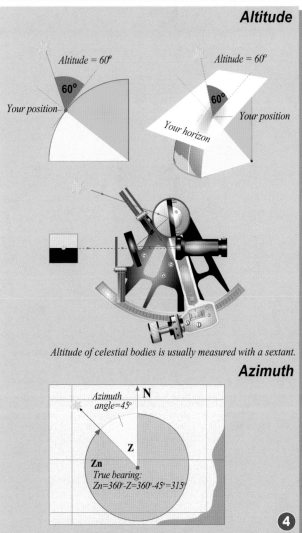

Altitude

Altitude of celestial bodies is usually measured with a sextant.

Azimuth

Azimuth angle=45°

True bearing:
$Zn=360°-Z=360°-45°=315°$

4

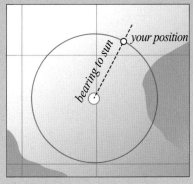

Anywhere on this circle you will measure the same altitude.

your position

GP (found in a nautical almanac)

The GP is the centre of a circle representing a constant altitude of the sun.

5

By observing (measuring) the sun's altitude you find that you are somewhere on a defined circle around the Sun's GP. From a nautical almanac you can find the position of the GP and the radius can be figured. With the help of a compass you find and mark off the bearing through the GP. Your position is where

this line intersects the circle. This method would require very large charts or charts scaled way too small as this circle could have a radius of several thousand nautical miles. ***Therefore we must take a little detour in order to find our position...***

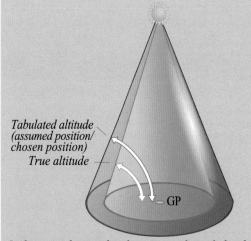

Tabulated altitude (assumed position/ chosen position)

True altitude

GP

In this example true altitude is greater than tabulated altitude at the assumed position. We have to be closer to the GP than the assumed position in order to get a greater altitude. We have to be on a position line (red circle) which is closer to the sun. (One nautical mile for every minute in altitude difference.)

The position lines are always 90° on the bearing to the sun - they can be seen as tangents to the circle at the bearing line.

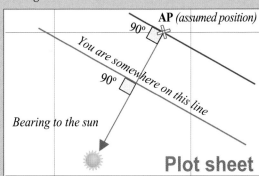

AP (assumed position)

90°

You are somewhere on this line

90°

Bearing to the sun

Plot sheet

On a large scale plot sheet, parts of a circle are drawn as straight lines (red and green position lines) because they are tiny parts of huge circles. The red position line will, along with a new observation, give us our position where these position lines intersect.

6

We measure the altitude of the sun and choose a position within 100 M of our actual position. This is called the ***assumed position*** and is chosen on the closest whole degree of latitude and a latitude adapted to the tables (shown further on in the book). Referring to the almanac and tables you can find out what the sun's altitude and true bearing ***should have been*** at that position at that precise time. This

is compared to your own observation. With a little chartwork the difference between these altitudes will give you a ***position line***. You have to make a new observation in order to get another position line. The interaction of these two position lines will give you your position. ***This is the principle of celestial navigation.***

Hour Angles

The sun's GP moves westward with 15° per hour, using 24 hrs to complete 360°. It moves slowly between 23½° north and 23½° south depending on the time of year. The sun's angle from the equator is called, as mentioned, declination, d.

The GP's distance in degrees from the 0-meridian (Greenwich) is called *Greenwich Hour Angle, GHA*. You can think of GHA as the sun's "longitude". Nautical almanacs give you declination and GHA for every hour, every day of the year.

The distance in degrees between your longitude and the sun's longitude is called *Local Hour Angle, LHA*. It is measured *towards the west* from your longitude to the sun's longitude.

Both these angles are measured *westward* from the 0-meridian from 0° to 360° as compared to the longitude which is measured from 0° to 180° east or west of the 0-meridian.

LHA is used along with latitude to enter the tables which will give you the sun's altitude at the assumed position. *The reason for using assumed position and not DR (dead reckoning) position, is because most tables are set up with whole degrees of latitude and LHA to limit their size.*

Time is referred to as **UTC** (Coordinated Universal Time) or GMT (Greenwich Mean Time) in the almanacs, but UTC will take over as the new norm.

LHA is found to the *nearest whole degree* based on GHA and assumed longitude. You enter the *Sight Reduction Tables* (Pub. no.249) with LHA, declination and assumed latitude. You then find the sun's *bearing* (Azimuth) and the sun's *altitude* you would have observed if you had been at your assumed position.

This altitude is compared to the one you found with the sextant. If true altitude is greater, you mark the difference (1' =1 M) *towards* the sun. If true altitude is less, you mark the difference *away* from the sun. A line through this new point, 90° on the direction to the sun, will be your new position line (fig. 6).

It is very important that you are able to find the correct LHA. It might be a good idea to make a drawing in order to visualize your work. It is easy to become confused, but if you follow the simple rules in fig. 8, you will get it right.

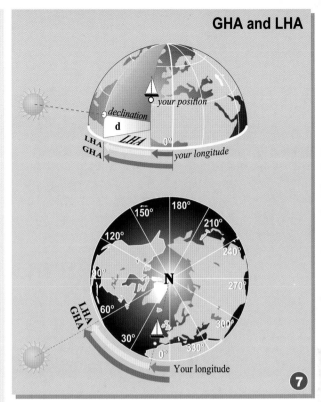

❼

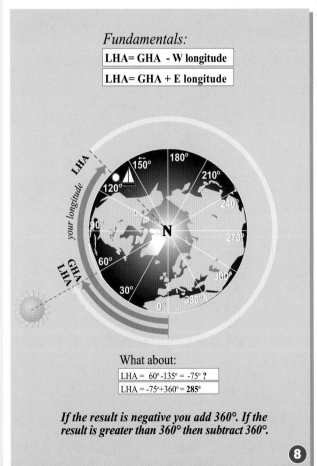

Fundamentals:

LHA= GHA - W longitude

LHA= GHA + E longitude

What about:

LHA = 60°-135° = -75° ?

LHA = -75°+360° = **285°**

If the result is negative you add 360°. If the result is greater than 360° then subtract 360°.

❽

Noon sight

The sun is at its highest at midday. It is due south (bearing 180°) or due north (bearing 360°). If you measure the altitude at the precise moment the sun is at its highest, you can find your latitude the easy way. After finding the declination from the almanac you work out the latitude. This is the simplest form of celestial navigation.

When the sun is observed at its highest it is located above the meridian at your location. The sun is in *your meridian*, we have a *meridian passage* or a *culmination*.

Note that the formula for latitude will change for different combinations of latitude and declination. Fig. 9 shows how the formula is derived for 3 different incidents. You don't have to memorize them but it is important that you chose the right one when figuring the latitude. Note also that you can't determine your position with just *one* observation. You have a position line you can combine with the next observation - often a few hours later. On the other hand if you use stars, planets or the moon in addition to the sun, several position lines can be found in a short time-span.

Because the distance to the sun is vastly greater than the radius of the earth, your line of sight to the sun and the line from the centre of the earth to the sun, through the GP, are defined as parallel. This is illustrated with two suns in the fig.

MZD = Meridional Zenith Distance is defined as 90 degrees minus the sun's altitude. We also find that MZD is the angle between the two lines from the earth's centre to the sun and our position.

By *same name* we mean that both latitude and declination are either north or south. *Opposite name* (the same as *contrary name*) means that latitude is south and declination is north or the other way around.

  h = altitude

  d = declination

  b = latitude

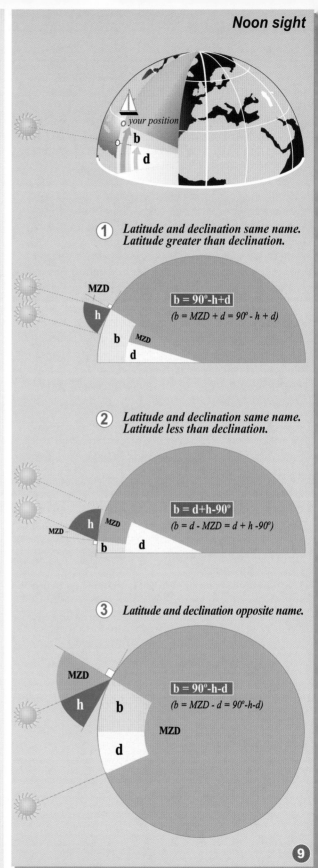

① *Latitude and declination same name. Latitude greater than declination.*

$$b = 90° - h + d$$
$$(b = MZD + d = 90° - h + d)$$

② *Latitude and declination same name. Latitude less than declination.*

$$b = d + h - 90°$$
$$(b = d - MZD = d + h - 90°)$$

③ *Latitude and declination opposite name.*

$$b = 90° - h - d$$
$$(b = MZD - d = 90° - h - d)$$

⑨

Measuring sun's altitude

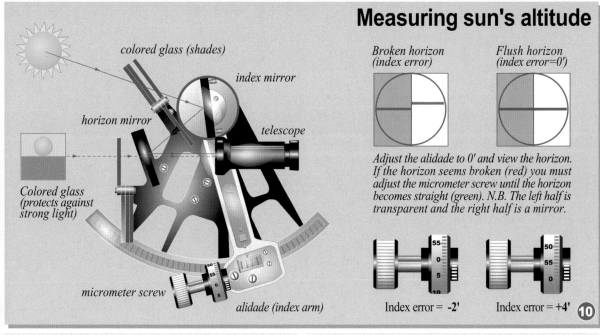

colored glass (shades)

index mirror

horizon mirror

telescope

Colored glass
(protects against
strong light)

micrometer screw

alidade (index arm)

Broken horizon
(index error)

Flush horizon
(index error=0')

Adjust the alidade to 0' and view the horizon. If the horizon seems broken (red) you must adjust the micrometer screw until the horizon becomes straight (green). N.B. The left half is transparent and the right half is a mirror.

Index error = **-2'**   Index error = **+4'**

⑩

Before using the sextant you must note the ***index error***. All sextants have an index error, especially plastic instruments which have to be checked regularly. When you have achieved an unbroken line as shown above, you note the index error. Just remember that index error is what you have to add or subtract in order to get 0.0' In the first example you have to subtract 2' and in the second you have to add 4' to get 0.0'. The index error is the same for any angle. It can change however and it is advisable to check the index error before any observation.

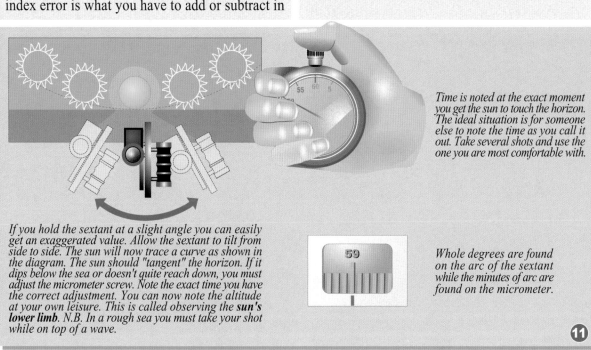

Time is noted at the exact moment you get the sun to touch the horizon. The ideal situation is for someone else to note the time as you call it out. Take several shots and use the one you are most comfortable with.

*If you hold the sextant at a slight angle you can easily get an exaggerated value. Allow the sextant to tilt from side to side. The sun will now trace a curve as shown in the diagram. The sun should "tangent" the horizon. If it dips below the sea or doesn't quite reach down, you must adjust the micrometer screw. Note the exact time you have the correct adjustment. You can now note the altitude at your own leisure. This is called observing the **sun's lower limb**. N.B. In a rough sea you must take your shot while on top of a wave.*

Whole degrees are found on the arc of the sextant while the minutes of arc are found on the micrometer.

⑪

Find a secure place to stand. Hold the sextant in your right hand and move the ***alidade*** until you see the sun in the right half of the viewer. Move the alidade until you see the horizon as well. Fine-tune the alidade with the micrometer screw until the sun "tangents" the horizon as explained above. It might be difficult to find the sun to begin with, but with a little practice, preferably in variable conditions, you will soon get the hang of it.
N.B. Be sure to use correct filters in front of the mirrors. Unfiltered sunlight may damage your eyes.

UTC, zone- and standard time

The earth has been divided into 24 time zones, each one 15°. Greenwich is zone 0 or Z (zulu). (Zone 12 is divided in two, +12 and -12, each one 7.5°.)

UTC (Coordinated Universal Time), formerly GMT (Greenwich Mean Time), is zone time at the Greenwich meridian. If you wish to find the zone time at other meridians, you must adjust for the longitude.

In the almanacs you will find a column named **TRANSIT** or **Mer. Pass.** on the *daily pages* for the sun. This is the time of *meridian passage* at Greenwich. You have to adjust for your longitude in order to find when the passage is in UTC at your position.

Standard time is used by some countries in order to utilize the daylight better, for example during the summer. They add 1 (some even 2) hours to zone time in order to have longer evenings.

Therefore calculated zone time is not always what the clocks of that area are showing. Something to keep in mind when planning to shop provisions or fuel or catch the last round at the local pub!

There will often be a certain amount of uncertainty concerning the different time zones.

Therefore it is a good idea to have one clock on board set to UTC and to use this for all of your tidal and astro calculations.

It might be an idea to operate with three time pieces, one for UTC, one for time at home port and one for standard time at your location, all of them well marked.

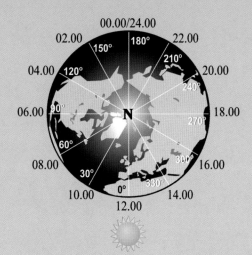

The sun's passage :	
24 hrs equals:	360°
1 hour equals:	15°
4 min equals:	1°
1 min equals:	15'

This is not totally correct as the sun's passage is not exactly 24hrs.

Example 1 (45° 00' W):

Zone time Greenwich		= **12.00**
- Hour adjustment 45°	= 45:15	= 3
= Zone time 45°00'W		= **09.00**

Example 2 (62° 30' E) :

Zone time Greenwich		= **14.20**
+ Hour adjustment 60°	= 60:15	= 4
+ Minute adjustment 2°30'	=150':15	= 10
= Zone time 62°30'E		= **16.10**

When converting an angle (e.g. longitude) to *time* you can use a table called **Conversion of Arc to Time** in the almanac.

45°	30°	15°	0°	15°	30°	45°
ZONE W	ZONE X	ZONE Y	ZONE Z	ZONE A	ZONE B	ZONE C
+3	+2	+1	**0**	-1	-2	-3

◄━━━ *W longitude* | *E longitude* ━━━►

Shown above are 7 of the 24 time zones. If you want to know UTC when the local time in zone +2 is 11, you must add 2 hrs. Time is 1300 UTC. When local time in zone -2 is 11, it is 11-2 = 0900 UTC and so forth.

Example (used in fig. 20 as well)
May 22, 1993 you are located at 24°47' W. From the almanac, under **TRANSIT**, you find that the meridian passage at the Greenwich meridian is 1157 UTC. *When is the meridian passage at our longitude?*

Meridian passage Greenwich	: 11.57 UTC
+W long 24°47' converted. to time:	1.39
= Meridian passage at our position:	**13.36 UTC**

Working a sight

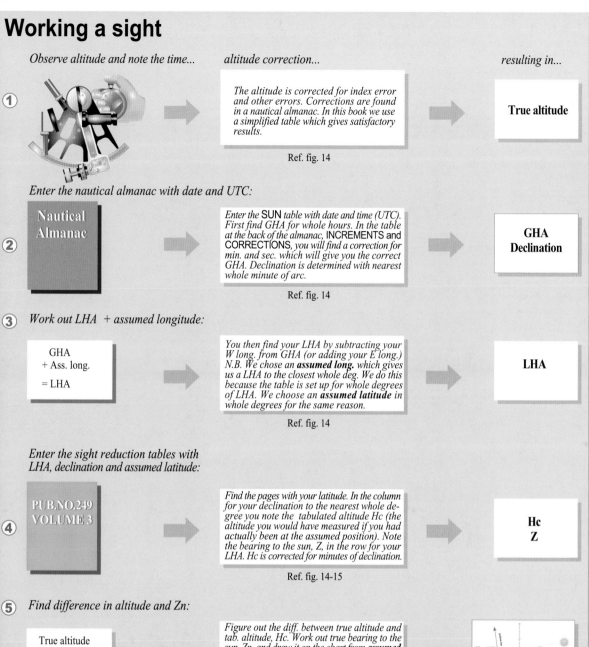

Observe altitude and note the time...

① *altitude correction...*

The altitude is corrected for index error and other errors. Corrections are found in a nautical almanac. In this book we use a simplified table which gives satisfactory results.

Ref. fig. 14

resulting in...

True altitude

② **Enter the nautical almanac with date and UTC:**

Nautical Almanac

Enter the SUN table with date and time (UTC). First find GHA for whole hours. In the table at the back of the almanac, INCREMENTS and CORRECTIONS, you will find a correction for min. and sec. which will give you the correct GHA. Declination is determined with nearest whole minute of arc.

Ref. fig. 14

GHA Declination

③ **Work out LHA + assumed longitude:**

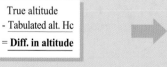

```
  GHA
+ Ass. long.
= LHA
```

You then find your LHA by subtracting your W long. from GHA (or adding your E long.) N.B. We chose an **assumed long.** which gives us a LHA to the closest whole deg. We do this because the table is set up for whole degrees of LHA. We choose an **assumed latitude** in whole degrees for the same reason.

Ref. fig. 14

LHA

④ **Enter the sight reduction tables with LHA, declination and assumed latitude:**

PUB.NO.249 VOLUME 3

Find the pages with your latitude. In the column for your declination to the nearest whole degree you note the tabulated altitude Hc (the altitude you would have measured if you had actually been at the assumed position). Note the bearing to the sun, Z, in the row for your LHA. Hc is corrected for minutes of declination.

Ref. fig. 14-15

Hc Z

⑤ **Find difference in altitude and Zn:**

```
  True altitude
- Tabulated alt. Hc
= Diff. in altitude
```

Figure out the diff. between true altitude and tab. altitude, Hc. Work out true bearing to the sun, Zn, and draw it on the chart from **assumed position**. Mark off a distance equal to difference in altitude, from assumed position **towards** or **away** from the sun. A line 90° on the bearing line to the sun is your position line.

Ref. fig. 15

Plot sheet

Ref. fig. 16

13

Taking accurate altitudes is the most difficult part of astro navigation. Understanding the theory in detail is really not necessary as long as you have a firm recipe of how to use the almanac and tables. It is, however, easier to spot mistakes if you have a certain understanding of the how and whys. Above you see an outline of the process from observation to plotting a position line. An observation of a noon sight is less complicated. Steps 3, 4 and 5 are not necessary, but observed latitude is plotted as a *horizontal* position line.

Example of an observation

1. True altitude

On May 22 1993 08.30.17 UTC the sun was "shot" with an altitude of 22°42.5' on passage from the Azores to Falmouth. The log shows 2573 and position by dead reckoning found to be N39°54', W25°29'. Index error of sextant is -2'. Height of eye is between 2.7 and 3 m.

Correcting sextant altitude: First enter the table on the right and note DIP for height of eye around 3 m. In the column for height of eye 2.9 m you will find **DIP = 3.0'**. DIP is a correction for the fact that we do not see the true horizon when height of eye is above sea level. This results in an apparent altitude of 22°37.5'. It's between 20° and 24° but closer to 20°. We note total corrections to be **14'** to the closest 0.5'. True altitude is worked out at **22°51.5'**. (Explanation of DIP and Total Corrections can be found on p. 74.)

2. Finding GHA

Enter an almanac for 1993 on the date in question, (May 22 1993 08.00 UTC). GHA is **300°50.9'** and declination is noted as **N 20°25'** (to the nearest whole minute). Correct GHA for 30 min. and 17 sec. as we found GHA for 08.00 and not 08.30.17. In the table INCREMENTS AND CORRECTIONS under **30 min** we note **7°34.3'** by 17 sec. This is added to GHA.

The correct GHA for May 22 1993 08.30.17 UTC is **308°25.2'**. N.B. Some almanacs show GHA for every 2 hrs and some every 6 hrs.

3. Calculating LHA

You *choose* your assumed longitude to be W20°25.2' in order to achieve LHA in whole degrees (283°). *Assumed latitude* is the closest whole degree which is N 40°. You now have the three values needed in order to enter the sight reduction tables and find tabulated altitude (Hc) and azimuth (Z). As mentioned earlier, this is the altitude and bearing you would have found if you were at the assumed position.

4. Finding tabulated altitude (Hc) and azimuth (Z)

Enter the sight reduction tables, Volume 2. Find the page for your chosen latitude N40° with the heading DECLINATION (15-29°) SAME NAME AS LAT because in this example both latitude and declination are northerly. Find the column for declination 20° (nearest whole degree to your declination). Follow the column down until you have the correct LHA. The values for LHA are found in both borders of the table. You can now note the values for Hc, d and Z.

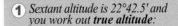

① *Sextant altitude is 22°42.5' and you work out true altitude:*

Sextant altitude:	22°	42.5'
Index error:		-2.0'
= Observed altitude:	22°	40.5'
+ DIP:		-3.0'
= Apparent altitude:	22°	37.5'
+ Total Corrections:		14.0'
= True altitude:	22°	51.5'

Date: *22.05.93*   Log: *1573*

Corrections to observed altitude

Height of eye	0.7m	1.3 m	2.0m	2.9m	3.9m
DIP	-1.5'	-2.0'	-2.5'	-3.0'	-3.5'
AA	>13°	15°	17°	20°	24°	31°	41°	59°	85°
TC	12'	12.5'	13'	13.5'	14'	14.5'	15'	15.5'	16'

AA=Apparent altitude   **TC**= Total Correct.

N.B. In many tables DIP correction is inluded in Total Corrections.

UTC-time at observation: 08.30.17   DR Position: N39° 54' | W25°29'

② *You then find GHA and declination in a nautical almanac:*

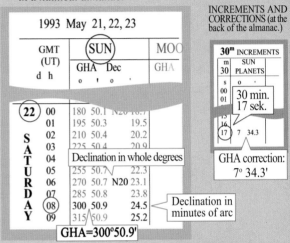

INCREMENTS AND CORRECTIONS (at the back of the almanac.)

1993 May 21, 22, 23

GMT (UT) d h	SUN GHA Dec	MOO GHA
22 00	180 50.1 N20 18.7	
01	195 50.3 19.5	
S 02	210 50.4 20.2	
A 03	225 50.4 20.9	
T 04	Declination in whole degrees	
U 05	255 50.7 22.3	
R 06	270 50.7 N20 23.1	
D 07	285 50.8 23.8	
A (08)	300 50.9 24.5	
Y 09	315 50.9 25.2	

GHA=300°50.9'

Declination in minutes of arc

30m INCREMENTS	
m 30	SUN PLANETS
s 00 01	30 min. 17 sek.
16 (17)	7 34.3

GHA correction: 7° 34.3'

③ *Calculate LHA:*

GHA whole hours:	300°	50.9'
+ GHA correction:	7°	34.3'
= GHA 08.30.17:	308°	25.2'
- W / + E latitude:	25°	25.2'
= LHA:	283°	00.0'

Assumed position
Choose latitude to the nearest whole degree.

N40°

Choose latitude to obtain LHA in whole degrees:

W25°25.2'

④ *Note tabulated altitude (Hc) and azimuth (Z):*

PUB.No.249, Volume 1-3, Sight Reduction Tables

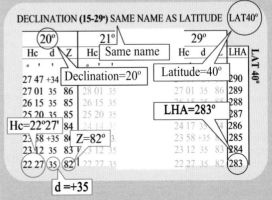

DECLINATION (15-29°) SAME NAME AS LATITUDE   LAT40°

20°		21°		29°		
Hc d	Z	Hc	Same name	Hc	d	LHA
27 47 +34		Declination=20°		Latitude=40°		290
27 01 35	86	28 01 35		27 01 35	86	289
26 15 35	85	26 15 35		26 15 35		288
25 20 35	85	25 20 35			LHA=283°	287
Hc=22°27'	84	24 14 35		24 17 35		286
23 58 +35	86	23 58 +35		23 58 +35		285
23 12 35	83	23 12 35		23 12 35	83	284
22 27 35	82	22 27 35		22 27 35	82	283

Z=82°

d =+35

⑭

PUB.No. 249, Volume 1-3

You must now correct Hc for the remaining 25' of declination which was 20°25' because we used the 20° column to find Hc. Enter the correction table at the back with d=35 in the horizontal row and 25' in the vertical row. Note 15' which you add to Hc. It doesn't matter if you switch the numbers. The answer is the same. Try it!

N.B. Remember that the **d**-correction is *added to* Hc if *same name* and subtracted if *contrary name*.

Same name: Declination and latitude both N or S

Contrary name = Opposite name: Declination N and latitude S or the other way around.

5. Calculating altitude difference and plotting the result (intercept)

Tabulated altitude equals 22°42'. True altitude turns out to be 9.5' greater than tabulated altitude. This means that assumed position has to be moved 9.5 M *towards* the sun. Usually we use a special chart, *plot sheet*, covering a small area showing only the grid. The plot sheet covers a small area (large scale) and is used along with a planning chart covering large areas (small scale). Here is where you transfer your observations from your plot sheet as your passage progresses.

☐ On the plot sheet mark 9.5 M towards the sun from assumed position.

☐ Draw a line through the end , k, 90° to the sun's bearing. This is your *position line* at 08.30.17 UTC.

☐ Move the sun's bearing parallel through your estimated position (DR) and find your *apparent position* where this line intersects the position line.

How to make a plot sheet

Start by drawing a line of latitude in the middle of the sheet. This would be the average of the area you wish to cover (here 40°). Draw meridians at right angles to the line of latitude. If you choose 60 mm as the distance between the meridians, *each mm* will represent *1 minute of arc*.

Draw a line through the intersection between a meridian and the line of latitude (A) at an angle equal to that of the latitude (here 40°). Place one leg of the dividers at A and the other at (B) where the line intersects the next meridian. Draw the circle. Where the circle intersects the line through A, you draw new parallel lines of latitude - in this case 41° and 39°.

Compass roses can be copied and pasted on the sheet. Self adhesive roses can be purchased as well. Divide up the deg. of latitude as shown. *(1 unit of latitude = 1 unit of longitude/cos. latitude)*

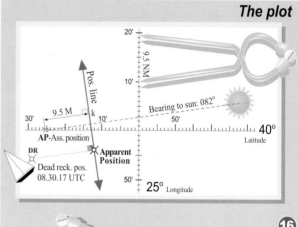

d	1	2	3	4	5		34	35	36
0	0	0	0				0	0	0
1	0	0	0				1	1	1
2	0	0	0						
3	0	0	0						
23	0	1	1				13	1	14
24	0	1	1				14	14	14
25	0	1	1				14	15	15

TABLE 5.-Correction to Tabulated Altitude

15' are added to Hc in order to achieve correct tabulated altitude.

Hc corrected for the remaining 25' of declination:

Hc (tabulated alt.):	22°	27.0'
+ d-correction:		+15.0'
= **Hc corrected:**	22°	42.0'
- True altitude:	22°	51.5'
= **Alt. diff. (Intercept):**		-9.5'

Altitude Difference

⑮

The plot

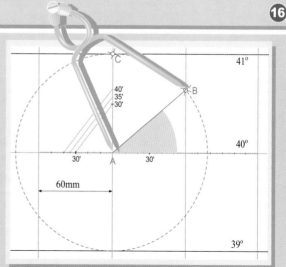

⑯

Latitude is divided by first halving a degree. Draw the line from this point to 30' on a degree of longitude. Draw parallels to the corresponding minutes of longitude as shown in the diagram. **⑰**

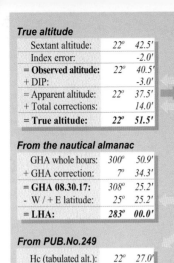

Sight reduction sheet

True altitude

Sextant altitude:	22°	42.5'
Index error:		-2.0'
= Observed altitude:	22°	40.5'
+ DIP:		-3.0'
= Apparent altitude:	22°	37.5'
+ Total corrections:		14.0'
= True altitude:	22°	51.5'

AA=Apparent altitude **TC**= Total corrrections

Height of eye	0.7m	1.3 m	2.0m	2.9m	3.9m				
DIP	-1.5'	-2.0'	-2.5'	-3.0'	-3.5'				
AA	>13°	15°	17°	20°	24°	31°	41°	59°	85°
TC	12'	12.5'	13'	13.5'	14'	14.5'	15'	15.5'	16'

From the nautical almanac

GHA whole hours:	300°	50.9'
+ GHA correction:	7°	34.3'
= GHA 08.30.17:	308°	25.2'
- W / + E latitude:	25°	25.2'
= LHA:	283°	00.0'

Assumed position

W 25°25.2'

Assumed longitude W/E

N 40°

Assumed latitude N/S

From PUB.No.249

Hc (tabulated alt.):	22°	27.0'
+ d - correction:		+15.0'
= Hc corrected:	22°	42.0'
- True altitude:	22°	51.5'
= Alt. diff. (intercept):		-9.5'

d = +35'   082° **Z**

+: *away from sun*
-: *towards sun*   082° **Zn**

Remember:

Correction for **d** is *added* if lat. and dec. have *same name* and *subtracted* if they have *opposite (contrary) name.* Position line to be moved *towards* the sun if true altitude is *greater* than tabulated altitude and *away* from the sun if true altitude is *less* than tabulated altitude.

True bearing Zn:

N latitude:	
LHA>180°	Zn= Z
LHA<180°	Zn= 360°-Z
S latitude:	
LHA>180°	Zn= 180°-Z
LHA<180°	Zn=180°+Z

Date: 22.05.93	Log:	1573
DR position:	N39° 54'	W25°29'
UTC at observation:		08.30.17
Declination:		N20° 25'
Log at local noon:		1599
Mer. Pass. Greewich.:		11.57 UTC
Estimert Mer. Pass.:		13.36 UTC

Latitude from the noon sight:

90° =	89°	60'
- True altitude:	70°	11'
= MZD:	19°	49'
+ Declination:	20°	27'
Latitude:	40°	16'

18

Above you see a sight reduction sheet with observations and calculations filled in. The sheet below can be copied for personal use or you can make your own. Different *Nautical Almanacs* are published every year. Sight reduction tables for air navigation, (Pub. 249, volume 1-3) were compiled for air navigation. Volume 1 is for stars, Volume 2 and 3 are intended for moon and planets but can also be used for stars. Vol. 2 covers latitudes 0-40°, Vol. 3 latitudes 39-89° (both north and south). Vol.1 is valid for 5 years, Vol.2 and 3 for ever.

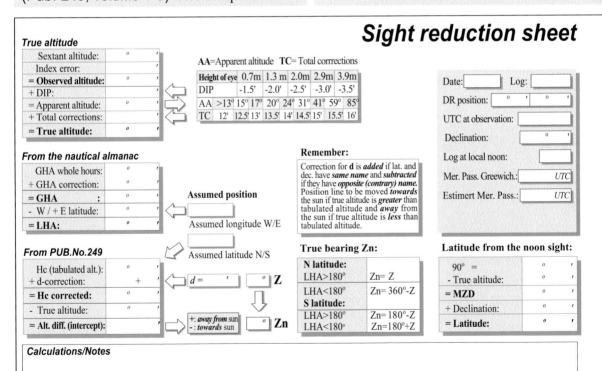

Sight reduction sheet

True altitude

Sextant altitude:	°	'
Index error:		'
= Observed altitude:	°	'
+ DIP:		'
= Apparent altitude:	°	'
+ Total corrections:		'
= True altitude:	°	'

AA=Apparent altitude **TC**= Total corrrections

Height of eye	0.7m	1.3 m	2.0m	2.9m	3.9m				
DIP	-1.5'	-2.0'	-2.5'	-3.0'	-3.5'				
AA	>13°	15°	17°	20°	24°	31°	41°	59°	85°
TC	12'	12.5'	13'	13.5'	14'	14.5'	15'	15.5'	16'

From the nautical almanac

GHA whole hours:	°	'
+ GHA correction:	°	'
= GHA :	°	'
- W / + E latitude:	°	'
= LHA:	°	'

Assumed position

Assumed longitude W/E

Assumed latitude N/S

From PUB.No.249

Hc (tabulated alt.):	°	'
+ d-correction:	+	'
= Hc corrected:	°	'
- True altitude:	°	'
= Alt. diff. (intercept):		'

d =   '   ° **Z**

+: *away from* sun
-: *towards* sun   ° **Zn**

Remember:

Correction for **d** is *added* if lat. and dec. have *same name* and *subtracted* if they have *opposite (contrary) name.* Position line to be moved *towards* the sun if true altitude is *greater* than tabulated altitude and *away* from the sun if true altitude is *less* than tabulated altitude.

True bearing Zn:

N latitude:	
LHA>180°	Zn= Z
LHA<180°	Zn= 360°-Z
S latitude:	
LHA>180°	Zn= 180°-Z
LHA<180°	Zn=180°+Z

Date:	Log:	
DR position:	°	°
UTC at observation:		
Declination:		° '
Log at local noon:		
Mer. Pass. Greewich.:		UTC
Estimert Mer. Pass.:		UTC

Latitude from the noon sight:

90° =	°	'
- True altitude:	°	'
= MZD	°	'
+ Declination:	°	'
= Latitude:	°	'

Calculations/Notes

NB! If you observe the suns *upper limb*, you have to find appropriate *altitude corrections* in an almanac.

19

Taking the Noon Sight

First you have to figure out when the sun *passes your meridian*. It is good enough to work it out to the closest minute. Start observing the sun a couple of minutes before calculated meridian passage. Don't make any adjustments to the sextant. Wait a minute before taking another shot. You will notice that the sun is a little bit higher in the sky. Keep this up until the sun no longer rises. You have taken a *noon sight*.

If you are unsure of the meridian passage, you can start observing as early as 13.30 UTC in this example.

Example: 22 May 1993

The meridian passage at Greenwich is found in a nautical almanac in the daily pages for the sun in the column named TRANSIT or MER.PAS. It turns out to be 11.57 UTC.

Because your pos is aprox. 25° W longitude the meridian passage at this longitude will occur about 1hr and 40 min. later, around 13.37 UTC. About 5 hrs after the morning shot. Let's assume an average speed of 5 kts. You will have covered around 25 M in those 5 hrs. If you mark this in the chart along your course line you will arrive at a probable longitude at 13.37 UTC. It turns out to be ca. 24°47'.

This results in a passage 1hr 39min 8sec, rounded to 1hr 39min, later. This will give you a slightly more accurate meridian passage of **13.36 UTC**.

The noon sight is noted as 70° which must be corrected as usual. *True altitude* turns out to be 70°10.8' which is rounded off to 70°11. If you subtract this from 90° and add the declination * you have found your *latitude*. This is a horizontal position line which is also a segment of a parallel of latitude.

You don't actually need a watch in order to find your latitude. When the sun seems high in the sky you start observing until the sun no longer climbs higher. When the sun seems to stabilize you have your noon sight. Be aware that you don't adjust the other way and follow the sun down again!

* *Latitude and declination both N, but latitude greater (fig. 9)*

Longitude converted to time (W24°47'):

24°=24 x 4min.= 96 min = 1hour 36 min	
+ Increment for 47' = 47: 15 = 3 min	
+ leftover 2' =120":15 =	8 sec
= Total 24°47'	**= 1 hour 39 min 8 sec**

Remember that 1°= 4min, 1'= 4 sec and 15"= 1sec.
N.B. You can use the table Conversion from Arc to Time in the back of the almanac to convert longitude (angle) to time easily.

22 May 1993

Meridian passage Greenwich:	=	11.57 UTC
- W longitude converted to time:	=	1.39
= Meridian passage W24°47':	**=**	**13.36 UTC**

The sun will be at its highest at the meridian passage. We keep measuring until it no longer rises. It seems to stay constant for a while before it starts sinking.

Sextant altitude correction:

Sextant altitude:	70°	00.0'
Index error:		-2.0'
= **Observed altitude:**	69°	58.0'
+ DIP:		-3.0'
= **Apparent altitude:**	69°	55.0'
+ Total corrections:		15.8'
= **True altitude:**	70°	10.8'

Date: 22.05.93   Log: 1599

Corrections to observed altitude

Height of eye	0.7m	1.3 m	2.0m	2.9m	3.9m
DIP	-1.5'	-2.0'	-2.5'	-3.0'	-3.5'
AA >13°	15°	17°	20°	24°	31°	41°	59°	85°
TC	12'	12.5'	13'	13.5'	14'	14.5'	15'	15.5'	16'

AA=Apparent altitude **TC**= Total corrections

Find latitude at local noon:

90° =	89°	60'
- True altitude:	70°	11'
= **MZD**	19°	49'
+ Declination:	20°	27'
= **Latitude:**	**40°**	**16'**

90° is often written as 89°60' in order to make it easier to subtract.

N.B. Declination changes from N20°25' to N20°27' in the hours between the shots. If you do not take this into consideration you will get an error of 2' equivalent to 2 M.

Plotting position lines

Draw your latitude on the chart or plot sheet (1). This is your new position line. Move the position line parallel from the morning observation (2) until it intersects your *DR (Dead reckoning position)* at midday (3). This is a calculated position based on your boat's course and distance travelled in a given time. The intersection between these lines is your new *observed position* (4) **OP** at midday.

DR position is found by marking off course and distance between the observations based on your apparent position AP, 08.30 UT. Track is assumed to be 048°. Distance covered derived from the log: 1599 - 1573 = 26 M. Accuracy in determining speed, course and offset due to wind and current is important for a good result.

Draw a new course line from observed position for the continued passage. Change course as often as you wish, as long as you keep track of your course and distance sailed.

If you take an evening shot you move the *midday latitude* (pos. line) parallel to where it intersects your DR pos. at the evening shot. (The whole process can be started afresh based on a DR position preferably within 100 M of your actual position.)

Common mistakes made when plotting

☐ You draw the sun's Azimuth from DR position instead of assumed position, drawing your position line 90° on this. Remember that assumed latitude is always a whole number of degrees and assumed longitude is chosen in order to round off LHA to the nearest whole degree.

☐ You use the same assumed position for multiple observations. Every observation (except for noon sights) will have a designated assumed position. Observations over time might well have the same assumed latitude, but almost never the same assumed longitude.

☐ You define distance from the longitude scale instead of the latitude scale. The error is nil at the equator but increases with increasing latitude.

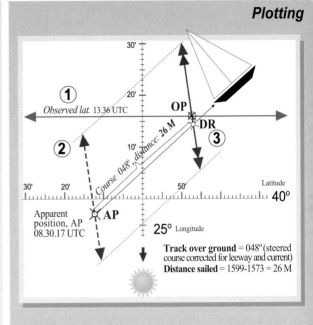

Observed lat. 13.36 UTC

Course 048°, distance: 26 M

Apparent position, AP 08.30.17 UTC

25° Longitude

Track over ground = 048° (steered course corrected for leeway and current)
Distance sailed = 1599-1573 = 26 M

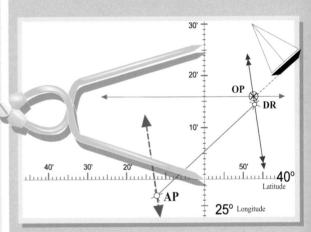

25° Longitude

Finding lat. and long. directly

If we could define the exact time of the meridian passage, we would be able to find our **longitude** at the noon sight. When the sun is in our meridian the LHA is 0°. At this point GHA is the same as our longitude. If we know the time of the meridian passage accurately enough, we can get our longitude from the GHA column in a nautical almanac.

When the sun is at its highest, the altitude seems stable for about 4 - 5 min. These minutes represent 1° (=60') which could mean an error of max. 60 M. This is way too inaccurate to determine longitude. But if you shot the sun about an hour before the noon sight and the same altitude about the same time after, you can find the sun's GHA by using the medium time for these two shots. *This will also be your longitude!*

N.B. It's a good idea to take several double shots around the noon sight, for example one at 12.37, one 5 min later and a third one 5 min after that again (make note of altitude and UTC). Take your noon sight as usual. Preset the sextant with the last altitude before your noon sight. A little before you expect the sun to be at this altitude again, for example at 14.30, you follow the sun until the altitude matches - make no adjustments. Note the time. Do the same with the other altitudes. Find the medium time for each of the three paired shots and finally the medium time for those three times.

This is the easiest way to find observed position. All you need is a nautical almanac, no tables and no need to do any plotting. You run the risk of clouds masking out the sun just as the sun gets close to preset altitudes and thus making it impossible to determine correct time. Therefore three sets of observations will increase your chances of at least getting one pair.

Normally this method of finding longitude is as accurate as the process shown in figs. 13 - 20.

N.B. You should correct for the distance travelled between shots with the same altitude. If you are stationary or travelling E or W you don't have to make corrections.

But if you are sailing **towards** the sun you have to adjust the preset altitude of the sextant by adding 1' for every M sailed since the first shot.

If you are sailing **away** from the sun you subtract 1' for every M.

Vessels doing 20 kn can experience large errors without corrections. At speeds of around 5 kts the errors are normally acceptable.

Longitude=GHA

When the sun is in the meridian LHA = 0°. GHA = your longitude.

Estimated meridian passage:	13.36.00 UTC

Sun's altitude before noon sight:	12.37.34 UTC
Same altitude after noon sight:	14.33.50 UTC
Medium time (12.37.34 and 14.33.50):	**13.35.42 UTC**
GHA 13.00 UTC:	15° 50.7'
+ Increment for 35 minutes =	8° 45.0'
+ Increment for 42 seconds =	10.4'
= **GHA 13.35.42 UTC = Your longitude:**	**24° 47.0'**

13.35.42
(Noon sight)

12.37.34   14.33.50

66° 10'   70° 00'   66° 04'

*We shoot the sun about an hour before the noon sight and note the exact time. After the noon sight has been taken the sextant is set to the first altitude. The time the sun reaches this altitude again is noted. The **meridian passage** is the average time between the first and last shot.*

Correction for N/S passage:

*Our example: In the course of 2 hrs you have covered 10 M doing 5 kts. With a track of 48° we can roughly say that you are 6 M further **from** the sun between the first and last shot. You therefore subtract 6' when presetting the sextant for the last shot.*

(66° 10' - 6' = 66° 04').

NB! At speeds around 5 kts you can drop this correction as long as you are aware that your position won't be the most accurate.

22

Corrections

What are the corrections we apply to sextant altitude?

☐ **Index error** - Inaccuracies with the sextant.

☐ **DIP** - You don't see the true horizon as your eyes are above the horizon. The altitude you measure is therefore too great due to the curve of the earth. DIP correction, which increases with height of eye, makes adjustments for this. DIP is always subtracted from sextant altitude.

☐ **Refraction** - The light from the sun is bent on its way through the atmosphere. At small altitudes this really becomes pronounced. Therefore avoid altitudes less than 6° and treat angles below 10° with caution (this applies to all heavenly bodies).

☐ **Semi-diameter** - The altitude of the sun is defined from its centre but it's easier to measure its lower or upper limb (applies to the moon as well, but not stars and planets).

☐ **Parallax** - We have assumed that the light from the heavenly bodies hit the earth as parallel lines (ref. fig. 9). This is not quite true. Sun, stars and planets are so far away that the correction for parallax is negligible and can be ignored. The Moon, however, is so much closer to the earth that a considerable correction is necessary.

In this book we use a combined table for DIP and altitude corrections for *lower limb*. Beware that the table set up in almanacs may differ. Note also that sextant altitude corrected for index error is *observed altitude*. Observed altitude corrected for DIP is called *apparent altitude*.

Altitude corrections incorporate corrections for refraction, parallax and semi-diameter. This is added to apparent altitude which gives you *true altitude*.

How accurate should you be when extracting information from the tables? Accuracy is important, but it is even more important to use the tables correctly so observed position is no more than 6 - 7 M out.

In the example in fig. 14 altitude correction was noted as 14.0' which is usually good enough. If you want more accurate calculations you could have used 13.8' instead (ref. fig. on right).

Results will improve with your routine, but you should always count on an error of a couple of miles. Remember as well that even if DR pos. should be 100 M off, you can achieve an accurate position as long as your observation and calculations are good.

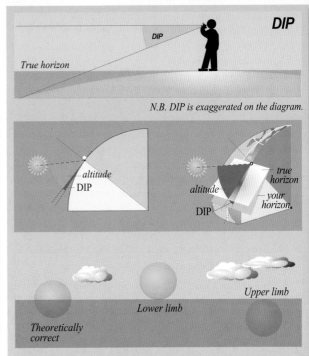

N.B. DIP is exaggerated on the diagram.

*Theoretically we should measure the centre of the sun. This is both difficult and not very practical. Therefore we usually measure the sun's altitude when its **lower limb** touches the horizon. If the sun's lower limb is obscured, we can use the **upper limb** instead. In that case you won't be able to use the correction table in this book. Enter a nautical almanac and the table called ALTITUDE CORRECTION under SUN with app.alt. and correct month. Find altitude correction in the column for UPPER LIMB.*

Interpolation

Height of eye	0.7m	1.3 m	2.0m	2.9m	3.9m
DIP	-1.5'	-2.0'	-2.5'	-3.0'	-3.5'
AA	>13° 15° 17°	20°	24°	31° 41° 59° 85°	
TC	12' 12.5' 13'	13.5'	14'	14.5' 15' 15.5' 16'	

*When reading the table above for apparent altitude 22°37.5' as shown in fig. 14, you can improve accuracy by **interpolation**.*

Total corrections (TC) for 24°:	*14.0'*
Total corrections (TC) for 20°:	*13.5'*
Differance for 4° (= 240') :	*0.5'*
Differance pr. minute (')	*= 0.5/240*

AA is 2° 37.5'= 157.5' more than 20° which gives correct increm.= 157.5 x 0.5 / 240 = 0.33'

Total corr. (TC) for 20°:	13.50'
Increment for 157.5' :	*0.33'*
TC for 22° 37.5' :	**13.88'**

Common errors...

There are many possibilities of making mistakes in celestial navigation. Some mistakes have greater consequences than others. The better you understand the principles of astronavigation the easier it is to spot mistakes and correct them in time. It is very important to find a systematic method in order to minimize the possibility of mistakes.

Use the Sight Reduction sheet in fig. 19, or make your own, in order to make a note of all observations and data. Keep these notes throughout the passage.

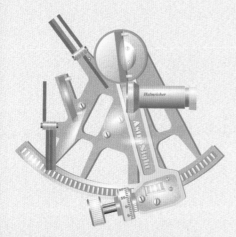

Incorrect calculations...

Mistakes are easily made when working with degrees and minutes for angles and hours, minutes and seconds for time.

1 deg. = 60 minutes of arc = 60'. But we operate with decimals of minutes for example 50.5' As for time we have the same problems but we are used to 1 hr = 60 min. and 1 min. = 60 sec.

Minutes and seconds should not be greater than 60! (Increase degrees, hours or minutes by one and leave the amount greater than 60 as leftover min. or sec.) Being *thorough* and *systematic* is the key to correct calculations.

Errors while taking the shot:

- *You haven't touched the sun on the horizon properly (fig. 11).*
- *You haven't managed to hold the sextant vertically (fig. 11).*
- *You haven't checked the sextant for index error (fig. 10).*
- *You haven't used correct UTC (fig. 12).*

Incorrect use of tables:

- *You've entered the almanac with the wrong date or month.*
- *You've referred to* ARIES *column instead of* SUN.
- *You've entered* CONTRARY NAME *instead of* SAME NAME *in the sight reduction tables.*
- *You've noted wrong declination in sight reduction tables.*
- *You've forgotten that the d-value is subtracted from altitude if* CONTRARY NAME *and added if* SAME NAME.

How to spot mistakes?

If you experience an altitude difference of more than 40' you should review your calculations. This discrepancy doesn't necessarily mean there is a mistake, however.

If the bearing to the sun is more than 180° at a morning shot, or less than 180° during an evening shot, you have done something wrong.

Incorrect calculations...

Arc (degrees/minutes)	Time (hours/min/sec.)
25.0'	25.0 sec.
+ 38.5'	+ 38.5 sec.
= 63.5'	= 63.5 sec.
= 1° 03.5'	= 1 min. 3.5 sec.

If we end up with more than 60 min we change the first 60 to 1 deg (arc) or 1hr (time) and keep the rest as minutes.

Subtracting degrees and minutes:

314° 18.5'	➡ 313° 78.5'
- 33° 52.0'	- 33° 52.0'
= 280° 26.5'	= 280° 26.5'

Calculation (same) to the right:
We borrow 1 deg. = 60 min. which we add to the 18.5' resulting in 78.5'. This simplifies the process.

Angles greater than 360°:

310° 42.5'	➡ 403° 10.5'
+ 92° 28.0'	- 360° 00.0'
= 402° 70.5'	= 43° 10.5'
= 403° 10.5'	

If you get angles greater than 360° you subtract 360° in order to get the correct angle.

Angles less than 0°:

-48°12.5'	➡	359° 60.0'
+ 360° 00.0'	or	- 48° 12.5'
= 311° 47.5'		= 311° 47.5'

If you get a negative angle (f.-ex. for LHA) you add 360° to the negative angle in order to get correct angle.

NB! Your results should never show numbers for min or sec larger than 60. Angles should not be greater than 360° or negative.

This and that

Sometimes there can be a problem seeing the sun (and other heavenly bodies) and a clear horizon at the same time. It's good to know that you don't always need a clear horizon. The diagram shows how an obscure horizon still allows you to take an accurate enough altitude.

You can measure altitude if islands or land are further away than the visible horizon and are clearly distinguishable from the horizon themselves.

Artificial horizon

Sometimes it is impossible to see the horizon. But it is still possible to take the sun's altitude using an **artificial horizon**. This is handy for finding your position far from the sea or just for practice without having to head out to sea.

There are many gadgets which can be attached to the sextant giving you an artificial horizon, e.g. the **bubble horizon**. Air pilots used these earlier. There are other smart gadgets which do the job as well.

In principle a bowl of water, oil, mercury or a similar liquid can be used. It must be placed on a firm, stable base protected from wind and reflection. This set-up would be difficult at sea, if not impossible.

Place your head so you see the sun's reflection in the middle of the fluid. Take the sextant and adjust it until you see *two* suns, one reflected from the fluid and one reflected from the horizon mirror.

In order to achieve a lower limb shot the lower limb in the horizon mirror is brought to tangent the upper limb of the reflection from the bowl of fluid by adjusting the micrometer.

N.B. The sextant altitude is corrected for index error, halved and corrected as usual, without DIP in this case.

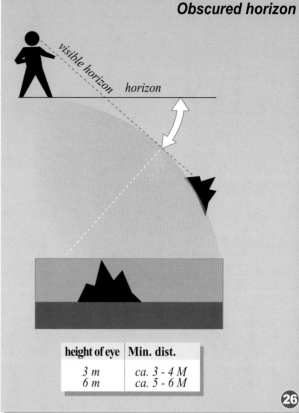

height of eye	Min. dist.
3 m	ca. 3 - 4 M
6 m	ca. 5 - 6 M

26

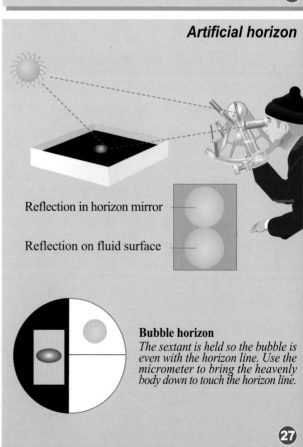

Reflection in horizon mirror

Reflection on fluid surface

Bubble horizon
The sextant is held so the bubble is even with the horizon line. Use the micrometer to bring the heavenly body down to touch the horizon line.

27

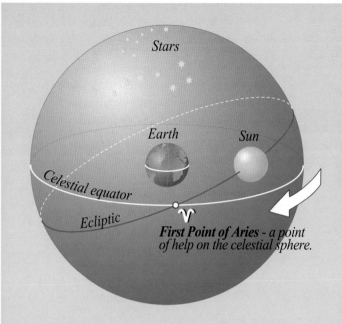

Stars

Earth   Sun

Celestial equator

Ecliptic

First Point of Aries - a point
of help on the celestial sphere.

Model for celestial navigation

*An imagined celestial sphere rotates around
a static earth once every 24 hrs. Sun, moon,
planets and stars are thought to be placed on
the sphere's surface. The sun, moon and planets
change positions relative to each other as well
as the stars. The stars are fixed on the sphere.*

28

Celestial navigation *presumes* that the earth is static in the centre of the universe and the *heavenly bodies* rotate around us on an *imagined* celestial sphere. The stars, which are infinitely far away, are glued on the sphere while the sun, moon and planets change positions relative to each other as well as to the stars.

As the earth's radius is miniscule compared to the celestial sphere, we imagine the eye of the observer at the centre of the earth. This simplification makes navigation using heavenly bodies much easier and removes the problem of slight inaccuracies.

Star observations

*In contrast to the sun, stars can only be observed 20 - 30 mins. twice a day, at dusk morning and evening. The advantage is that you have the opportunity to observe several stars in a short time. Thus you can find **observed position** with intersecting position lines without waiting for a later observation.*

Finding position with star observations

1. Find GHAϒ and work out assumed LHAϒ for the observation period.
2. Enter the sight reduction tables, Volume 1, with DR lat. and LHAϒ in whole degrees and choose three suitable stars to observe.
3. Set the sextant to the stars designated altitude and find them by looking for them in their designated true bearings (Zn).
4. Adjust the sextant so the stars touch the horizon. Note the correct time and altitude. Find true altitude by correcting for index error, DIP and refraction.
5. Find accurate LHAϒ for each star (closest whole degree). Enter the table again and find tabulated altitude, Hc and true bearing, Zn (Azimuth).
6. Correct the sextant altitudes and compare to tabulated altitudes. The difference is drawn on the chart along the Azimuth as shown in fig. 32.

*NB! You can also use Vol. 2 and 3 for stars in the same way you find your pos. with the sun but you must use altitude corrections for stars. The stars declination and **Sidereal Hour Angle**, SHA, is found in the almanac. The calculation is as described in fig. 38, with the help of a calculator.*

29

In order to avoid having to make tables for GHA for every star, tables have been made for the so called *First Point of Aries* as if it were a heavenly body. It is in fact only an *imagined point* on the celestial spheres which coincides with the point of *summer equinox*. The hour angle between the First Point of Aries and the different stars is constant. Thus for any given time we can find GHA for Aries (GHAϒ) and work out LHA for Aries (LHAϒ). With LHAϒ to the nearest degree and DR lat. you enter sight reduction tables Vol. 1 where you will find tabulated altitude and Azimuth, Zn, to a number of stars.

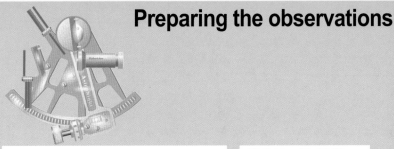

DR position 04.01 UTC:

N 41° 03' W 23° 30'

Working out LHA♈︎

GHA♈︎ 04.00:	300° 47.0'
Increment for 1 min.:	15.0'
GHA♈︎ 04.01:	301° 02.0'
- W DR longitude:	23° 30.0'
LHA♈︎ 04.01:	277° 32.0'

As we know that LHA increases 1° every 4 min (15° in an hr., 360° in 24 hrs.), we can create a list for LHA♈︎ in whole degrees

Time (UTC)	LHA♈︎	Time (UTC)	LHA♈︎
04.01	278°	04.17	282°
04.05	279°	04.21	283°
04.09	280°	04.25	284°
04.13	281°	04.29	285° etc.

*You can only observe the stars when it is dark enough for them to be visible while still being able to make out the horizon. You have about 20 - 30 min morning and evening, **twilight**, when you can take a shot. Times for **Civil Twilight** are found in the almanac.*
The limit of Civil Twilight occurs when the sun is 6° below the horizon. During Civil Twilight we have indirect light reflected from the upper atmosphere.

Note that different almanacs have different tables for finding Civil Twilight.

1993 May 21, 22, 23

GMT (UT)	ARIES	VE
d h	GHA	GH
	° '	
23 00	241 00.1	
01	255 13.3	
M 02	270 39.4	
O 03	285 50.4	
N 04	300 47.0	
D		

GHA♈︎ = 300° 47.0'

May 22 1993, on passage from the Azores to Falmouth, we make preparations for morning observations for May 23. From the almanac we find that Civil (not Nautical) Twilight is around 04.01 UT. There we find the time 02.29 which must be corrected by + 1 hr and 32 min for presumed long. of 23°. In the almanac you find that GHA♈︎ for 23/5 04.00 UT = 300° 47'. You set up the table for LHA♈︎ as shown above. This will cover the time you are interested in. Then enter the sight reduction table, Vol.1, on DR long. 41°N and LHA♈︎ from 277 to 279° and choose three suitable stars from the table.

From sight red. table, Vol. 1: ②

LHA♈︎	STAR	Hc	Zn
278°	Alpheratz	22° 47'	071°
279°	ANTARES	16° 26'	209°
280°	Alkaid	39° 48'	306°

Set the sextant to the designated altitude of the first star and look for it in the designated true bearing (Zn). When you find the star adjust the micrometer so it touches the horizon. Note the correct time and altitude. Repeat the process with the other two stars.

③④
The following observations were made:

Time (UTC)	STAR	Sextant altitude
04.02.16	Alpheratz	22° 47.5'
04.06.22	ANTARES	16° 27.5'
04.12.35	Alkaid	39° 44.0'

Corrections to altitudes: ④

	Alpheratz	ANTARES	Alkaid
Sextant altitude	22° 47.5'	16° 27.5'	39° 44.0'
Index error	- 2.0'	- 2.0'	-2.0'
= Observed altitude	22° 45.5'	16° 25.5'	39° 42.0'
- DIP	- 3.0'	- 3.0'	-3.0'
= Apparent altitude	22° 42.5'	16° 22.5'	39° 39.0'
- Refraction	- 2.6'	- 2.8'	- 0.9'
= True altitude	**22° 39.9'**	**16° 19.7'**	**39° 38.1'**

*N.B. Only choose stars with **tabulated altitude** greater than 10°, otherwise your refraction will be large and your altitude inaccurate. When a star has an altitude greater than 45°, you can omit correction for refraction (maximum error = 1' = 1 M).*

Choose the three stars marked with small "diamonds", **Alpheratz**, **ANTARES** and **Alkaid**. The diamonds indicate that there is a difference of 120° between their Azimuths. The position lines obtained from these stars will give good intersections. ANTARES written in capital letters, is a bright star. The other two are less bright. Make a note of the stars' tabulated altitude, Hc and Azimuth, Zn.

Working out difference in altitude

You must find GHA♈ for each of the three stars at their exact time of observation. You then choose your *longitude* (as with sun observations) ending up with LHA♈ to the *nearest whole degree*. Enter the sight reduction tables, Vol. 1, with assumed longitude and LHA♈ and find *tabulated altitude*, Hc, for each star.

You make note of the Azimuth (Zn) or *true bearing* of the three stars. Find the *difference* between true and tabulated altitude. Finally you determine if they are to be drawn as distances *towards* or *away from* the stars on your plotting sheet below.

N.B. Choose assumed longitude to coincide with the table you set up in fig. 30.

Start plotting the first star, Alpheratz (blue). Draw the star's Azimuth through your *assumed position* when observing that star. Mark 7.1 M from this position along the Azimuth *away from* the star. Finally draw a line 90° on the Azimuth at this point. *This is the position line derived from Alpheratz.*

Repeat the operation with the other two stars. You will find yourself in the triangle created by the three position lines. Usually you assume your position to be in the centre of the triangle. *If you are close to obstructions, always choose a point within the triangle which is closest to the obstacle! In this example your observed posion is:*

N41° 10.5' W23° 33.5'.

N.B. You can combine one or more position lines from stars with position lines from sun.

Just remember that you must move position lines parallel to compensate for any significant time between observations.

(5) Working out LHA♈:

	Alpheratz	ANTARES	Alkaid
Time (UTC)	04.02.16	04.06.22	04.12.35
GHA♈ (whole hours)	300° 47.0'	300° 47.0'	300° 47.0'
+ GHA♈ (min. + sec.)	34.1'	1° 35.7'	3° 09.3'
= GHA♈	301° 21.1'	302° 22.7'	303° 56.3'
- Assumed W longitude	23° 21.1'	23° 22.7'	22° 56.3'
= LHA♈	278° 00.0'	279° 00.0'	281° 00.0'

from almanac (fig.30)

to sight.red.table, Vol. 1

(6)

	Alpheratz	ANTARES	Alkaid
True altitude	22° 39.9'	16° 19.7'	39° 38.1'
- Tabulated altitude	22° 47.0'	16° 26.0'	39° 11.3'
Difference in altitude	- 7.1'	- 6.3'	27.1'
Azimuth (true bearing)	071°	209°	306°
	away	away	towards

NB! Position lines are moved **towards** the star when true altitude is greater than tabulated (+) and **away** when less than tabulated altitude (-).

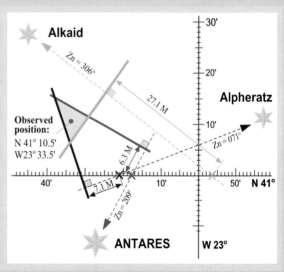

Assumed longitude is **N 41°** in this case.

Polaris (North Star)

Example:
May 23 1993, on passage from the Azores, Polaris is shot with an altitude of 41° 15' around 20.05 UTC. This altitude is corrected for index error, DIP and refraction.

Polaris	
Sextant altitude	*41° 15.0'*
Index error	*- 2.0'*
= Observed altitude	*41° 13.0'*
- DIP	*- 3.0'*
= Apparent altitude	*41° 10.0'*
- Refraction	*- 1.2'*
= True altitude	*41° 08.8'*

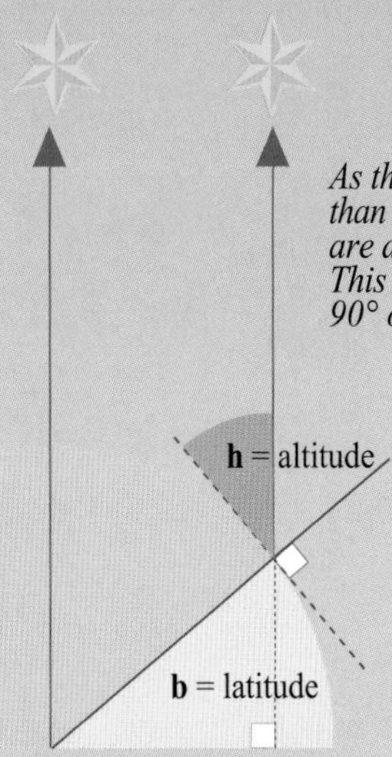

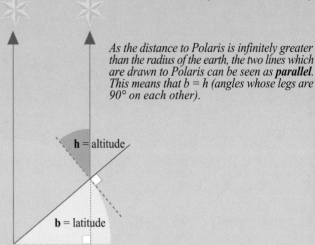

As the distance to Polaris is infinitely greater than the radius of the earth, the two lines which are drawn to Polaris can be seen as ***parallel****. This means that b = h (angles whose legs are 90° on each other).*

33

In the ***northern hemisphere*** there is a simple way to find your ***latitude*** with the help of ***Polaris***. Take the altitude, note the time to the nearest minute (close enough) and find true altitude. Then you find GHA♈ from the almanac and figure LHA♈. All the necessary corrections are found in the almanac under POLE STAR TABLES. ***If Polaris was always situated over the pole, its altitude would be identical to your latitude!*** But Polaris can be between 1 - 2° E or W of true north. Therefore a correction is needed.

Finding latitude from Polaris

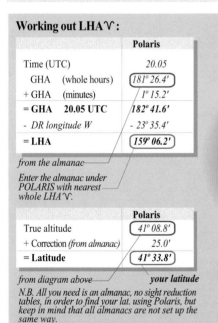

Working out LHA♈:

	Polaris
Time (UTC)	*20.05*
GHA (whole hours)	*181° 26.4'*
+ GHA (minutes)	*1° 15.2'*
= GHA 20.05 UTC	***182° 41.6'***
- *DR longitude W*	*- 23° 35.4'*
= LHA	***159° 06.2'***

from the almanac

Enter the almanac under POLARIS with nearest whole LHA♈.

	Polaris
True altitude	*41° 08.8'*
+ Correction *(from almanac)*	*25.0'*
= Latitude	***41° 33.8'***

from diagram above ***your latitude***

N.B. All you need is an almanac, no sight reduction tables, in order to find your lat. using Polaris, but keep in mind that all almanacs are not set up the same way.

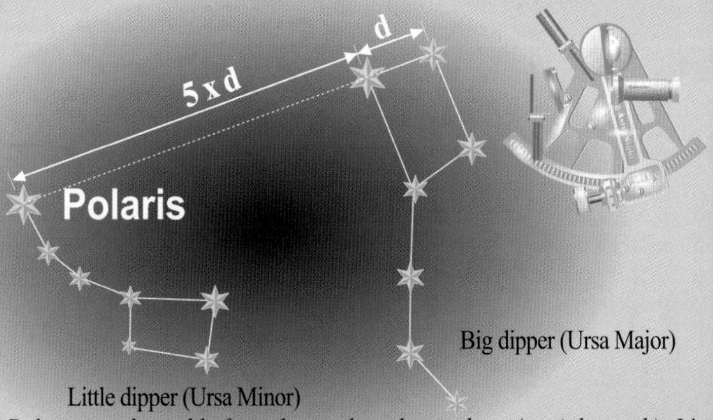

Polaris is only visible from the northern hemisphere (straight north): It's located in the constellation "Little Dipper" (Ursa Minor). If you extend the end wall of the Big Dipper (Ursa Major) about 5 times, you will find Polaris = Stella Polaris = North Star.

34

As Polaris is of medium brightness, it can sometimes be hard to spot. At twilight adjust your sextant to your ***DR latitude***. Aim it towards the north and spot Polaris. You can use Polaris to adjust your compass as well, as its true bearing is supposed to be 360° = (0°). For more accurate bearings use a table called AZIMUTH OF POLARIS in the almanac, where you can make corrections for LHA♈ and your latitude during observation.

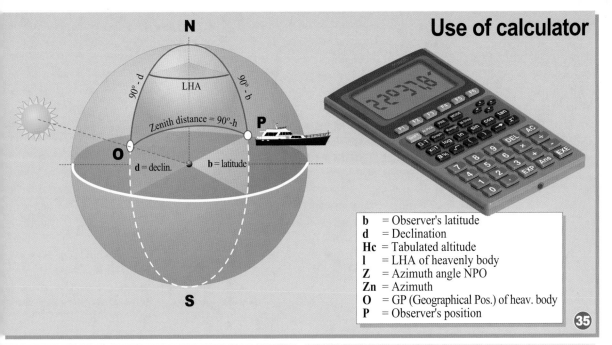

b	= Observer's latitude
d	= Declination
Hc	= Tabulated altitude
l	= LHA of heavenly body
Z	= Azimuth angle NPO
Zn	= Azimuth
O	= GP (Geographical Pos.) of heav. body
P	= Observer's position

35

We find our position line by solving the so called *astronomical triangle*, OPN (or OPS in the southern hemisphere). The Sight Reduction Tables are built up with these calculations. By using a *calculator* you can do without these tables. You observe the altitude as normal, and find the *GHA* and *declination* of the heavenly body from the almanac. Now you can use *DR position* as reference, since whole degrees of latitude and LHA are no longer required for the sight reduction tables. Altitude and Azimuth are found using the formulae below.

Formulae you can use
N.B. There are other formulae which will give the same results.

Altitude calculation:

$$Hc = \arcsin (\sin b \times \sin d + \cos b \times \cos d \times \cos l)$$

Azimuth calculation:

$$Z = \arccos ((\sin d - \sin b \times \sin h)/\cos b \times \cos h)$$

*N.B. For N lat., S dec. is entered on the calculator with negative value. For S lat., N dec. is entered on the calculator with negative value (sin b x sin d **is negative if opposite names**). You must also know how the calculator handles degrees and minutes. Decimals of degrees is most common.*
(Examples: 0.54° = 60' x 0.54 =32.4', 25' = 25/60 = 0.417°, 56.2' = 52.6/60 = 0.877°)

N latitude:	LHA>180 °: Zn = Z,	LHA<180 °: Zn = 360 °- Z
S latitude:	LHA>180 °: Zn = 180°- Z,	LHA<180 °: Zn = 180 °+ Z

*It might be difficult to imagine that zenith **distance = 90° - h**. If you view the great circle through O and P you should be able to see that this is correct (we assume that the two lines to the sun are parallel).*

36

Two sides in this *spherical triangle* can be determined by the heavenly body's *declination* and the observer's *DR latitude*. As the angle **ONP** equals our LHA, the altitude, **Hc**, and Azimuth, **Zn**, can be calculated using the formulae above. N.B. It is not necessary to understand how the formulae are derived, as long as they are used correctly. Try to calculate the examples on the following two figs. Be accurate when transforming decimals of degrees to minutes and seconds and vice-versa. Pay attention to the declination, it must be *negative* if *opposite name (=contrary name)*.

Calculating sun observations

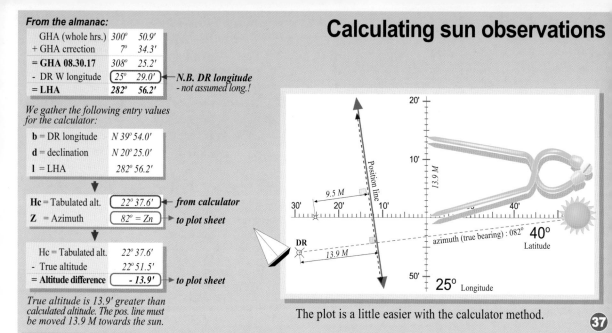

From the almanac:

GHA (whole hrs.)	300°	50.9'
+ GHA crrection	7°	34.3'
= GHA 08.30.17	308°	25.2'
- DR W longitude	25°	29.0'
= LHA	282°	56.2'

N.B. DR longitude - not assumed long.!

We gather the following entry values for the calculator:

b = DR longitude	N 39° 54.0'
d = declination	N 20° 25.0'
l = LHA	282° 56.2'

Hc = Tabulated alt.	22° 37.6'	← *from calculator*
Z = Azimuth	82° = Zn	*to plot sheet*

Hc = Tabulated alt.	22° 37.6'
- True altitude	22° 51.5'
= **Altitude difference**	- 13.9'

to plot sheet

True altitude is 13.9' greater than calculated altitude. The pos. line must be moved 13.9 M towards the sun.

The plot is a little easier with the calculator method.

Let's try the morning observation from figs. 14 - 16. In this case we have to use the **DR longitude** instead of assumed longitude in order to find correct LHA. **Declination** is found in the almanac, and along with **DR longitude** and LHA makes up the entry values for the work on the calculator. With the DR as

starting point, a line is drawn with the true bearing to the sun (083°). The **position line** is drawn 90° to this line at the correct distance, 13.9 M, from DR. We notice that this position line is almost exactly in the same place as the one derived from the sight reduction tables in fig. 16.

Calculating star observations

Finding LHA:

	Alpheratz	ANTARES	Alkaid
GHA♈	301° 21.1'	302° 22.7'	303° 56.3'
+ SHA	357° 59.1'	112° 44.3'	153° 10.3'
= GHA	659° 20.2'	415° 07.0'	457° 06.6'
subtract 360° . . .	- 360° 00.0'	- 360° 00.0'	- 360° 00.0'
= GHA	299° 20.2'	55° 07.0'	97° 06.6'
- W DR longitude	23° 30.0'	23° 30.0'	23° 30.0'
= LHA	275° 50.2'	31° 37.0'	73° 36.6'

to calculator along with DR longitude

	Alpheratz	ANTARES	Alkaid
Declination from almanac	N 29° 03.2'	S 26° 25.1'	N 49° 20.9'
True altitude	22° 39.9'	16° 19.7'	39° 38.1'
Calculated altitude	22° 42.2'	16° 26.2'	39° 33.5'
Altitude difference	- 2.3'	- 6.5'	4.6'
Azimuth angle (Z)	071°	151°	54°
Azimuth (Zn)	071°	209°	306°

to plot sheet: away from star — *away* — *towards* — *to plot sheet*

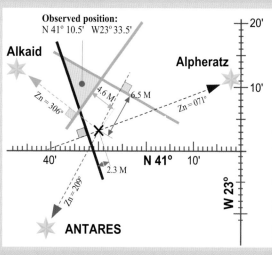

Observed position:
N 41° 10.5'   W23° 33.5'

DR position 04.01 UTC: N41° 03' W23° 30'

When using a **calculator** instead of sight reduction tables when observing stars, you have to find the star's LHA instead of LHA♈. First you find **SHA** (sidereal hour angle) for each star in the **STAR** table in the almanac. The table refers to the first day of every month, so interpolation gives greater accuracy - even

if SHA changes very little from one month to the next. SHA is added to GHA♈ in order to find GHA. This way there is no need to make separate tables for each star. LHA is found by adding or subtracting your DR longitude. *As you can see we get the same result as in fig. 32.*

Tables and formulae

$$\text{Speed in knots} = \frac{\text{Distance in nautical miles}}{\text{Time in hours}}$$

$$\text{Speed in knots} = \frac{\text{Distance in nautical miles x 60}}{\text{Time in minutes}}$$

$$\text{Speed in knots*} = \frac{\text{Distance in meters x 2}}{\text{Time in seconds}}$$

$$\text{Distance in M} = \text{Speed in knots x time in hours}$$

$$\text{Distance in M} = \frac{\text{Speed in knots x time in min.}}{60}$$

$$\text{Distance in meters*} = \frac{\text{Speed in knots x time in sec.}}{2}$$

$$\text{Time in hours} = \frac{\text{Distance in nautical miles}}{\text{Speed in knots}}$$

$$\text{Time in minutes} = \frac{\text{Distance in nautical miles x 60}}{\text{Speed in knots}}$$

$$\text{Time in seconds*} = \frac{\text{Distance in meter x 2}}{\text{Speed in knots}}$$

nautical mile (M) to km

nm	1	2	5	10	15	20	25	30	35	40	45	50
km	1.9	3.7	9.3	18.5	27.8	37.0	46.3	55.6	64.9	74.1	83.3	92.6

km to nautical mile (M)

km	1	2	5	10	15	20	25	30	35	40	45	50
nm	0.54	1.08	2.70	5.40	8.10	10.8	13.5	16.2	18.9	21.6	24.3	27.0

foot to meter

foot	1	2	5	10	15	20	25	30	35	40	45	50
m	0.30	0.61	1.52	3.05	4.57	6.10	7.62	9.14	10.7	12.2	13.7	15.2

meter to foot

m	1	2	3	4	5	6	7	8	9	10	15	20
foot	3.28	6.56	9.82	13.1	16.4	19.7	23.0	26.3	29.5	32.8	49.2	65.6

NB! 12 inches = 12" = 1 fot = 1' = 30.5 cm

inch to cm

"	1	2	3	4	5	6	7	8	9	10	11	12
cm	2.54	5.08	7.62	10.2	12.7	15.2	17.8	20.3	22.9	25.4	27.9	30.5

cm to inch

cm	1	2	5	6	7	8	9	10	20	30	40	50
"	0.39	0.79	1.97	2.36	2.76	3.15	3.54	3.94	7.87	11.8	15.8	19.7

* The factor 2 is determined as follows:

$$1 \text{ knot} = \frac{1 \text{ nautical mile}}{1 \text{ hour}} = \frac{1852 \text{ m}}{60 \times 60 \text{ s}} = 0.51 \text{ m/s}$$

1 knot is around 0.5 m/s or 1 m/s is roughly 2 kn!

Boat speed

Time used covering 1 minute of arc = 1 nautical mile

Min	1	2	3	4	5	6	7	8	9	10	11	12
Sec.				Boat speed in knots								
0	60.0	30.0	20.0	15.0	12.0	10.0	8.57	7.50	6.67	6.00	5.45	5.00
5	55.4	28.8	19.5	14.7	11.8	9.86	8.47	7.42	6.61	5.95	5.41	4.97
10	51.4	27.7	19.0	14.4	11.6	9.73	8.37	7.35	6.55	5.90	5.37	4.93
15	48.0	26.7	18.5	14.1	11.4	9.60	8.28	7.27	6.49	5.85	5.33	4.90
20	45.0	25.7	18.0	13.9	11.3	9.47	8.18	7.20	6.43	5.81	5.29	4.86
25	42.4	24.8	17.6	13.6	11.1	9.35	8.09	7.13	6.37	5.76	5.26	4.83
30	40.0	24.0	17.1	13.3	10.9	9.23	8.00	7.06	6.32	5.71	5.22	4.80
35	37.9	23.3	16.7	13.1	10.8	9.11	7.91	6.99	6.26	5.67	5.18	4.77
40	36.0	22.5	16.4	12.9	10.6	9.00	7.83	6.92	6.21	5.63	5.14	4.74
45	34.3	21.8	16.0	12.6	10.4	8.89	7.74	6.86	6.15	5.58	5.11	4.71
50	32.7	21.2	15.7	12.4	10.3	8.78	7.66	6.79	6.10	5.54	5.07	4.68
55	31.3	20.6	15.3	12.2	10.1	8.67	7.58	6.73	6.05	5.50	5.03	4.65
60	30.0	20.0	15.0	12.0	10.0	8.57	7.50	6.67	6.00	5.45	5.00	4.62
	1	2	3	4	5	6	7	8	9	10	11	12

Example:
You time a *measured mile* (1 nm) at 8 min and 30 sec. Enter the *column* for *8 min* and follow it down to the *row* for *30 sec*. Here you find the *boat speed* at 7.06 kn.

Index